CHRISTOPHER COLUMBUS'S EPOCH

Norma Iris Pagan Morales

ISBN 978-1-959895-58-9 (paperback)
ISBN 978-1-959895-57-2 (ebook)

Printed in the United States of America

WESTPOINT
PRINT AND MEDIA

DEDICATION

Dedicated to my sister Adelin for always being there for me.

OVERVIEW

Christopher Columbus, the explorer credited with the European discovery of Puerto Rico.

Juan Ponce de León, Santervás de Campos, Valladolid, Spain, was the first governor of Puerto Rico. His grandson Juan Ponce de Leon II was the first <u>indigenous</u> governor of Puerto Rico.

On September 24, 1493, Christopher Columbus set sail on his second voyage with 17 ships and 1,200 to 1,500 soldiers from Cádiz.

On November 19, 1493, he landed on the island, naming it San Juan Bautista in honor of Saint John the Baptist. The first European colony, Caparra, was founded on August 8, 1508, by Juan Ponce de León, a lieutenant under Columbus, who was greeted by the Taíno Cacique Agüeybaná and who later became the first governor of the island.

Ponce de Leon was actively involved in the Higuey massacre of 1503 in Hispaniola, present-day Dominican Republic.

In 1508, Sir Ponce de Leon was chosen by the Spanish Crown to lead the conquest and slavery of the Taíno Indians for gold mining operations.

The following year, the colony was abandoned in favor of a nearby islet on the coast, named Puerto Rico, Rich Port, which had a suitable harbor.

In 1511, a second settlement, San Germán was established in the southwestern part of the island. According to the "500TH Florida Discovery Council Round Table", on March 3, 1513, Juan Ponce de León, organized and commenced an expedition, with a crew of 200, including women and free blacks, departing from "Punta Aguada" Puerto Rico.

Puerto Rico was the historic first gateway to the discovery of Florida, which opened the door to the settlement of the southeastern United States.

They introduced Christianity, cattle, horses, sheep, the Spanish language and more to the land, Florida, that later became the United States of America. This settlement occurred 107 years before the Pilgrims landed.

During the 1520s, the island took the name of Puerto Rico while the port became San Juan.

The Spanish settlers established the first encomienda system, under which natives were distributed to Spanish officials to be used as slave labor.

On December 27, 1512, under pressure from the Roman Catholic Church, Ferdinand II of Aragon issued the Burgos' Laws, which modified the encomienda into a system called repartimento, aimed at ending the exploitation.

The laws prohibited the use of any form of punishment toward the indigenous people, regulated their work hours, pay, hygiene, and care, and ordered them to be catechized.

In 1511, the Taínos revolted against the Spanish; cacique Urayoán, as planned by Agüeybaná II, ordered his warriors to drown the Spanish soldier Diego Salcedo to determine whether the Spaniards were immortal.

After drowning Salcedo, they kept watch over his body for three days to confirm his death. The revolt was easily crushed by Ponce de León and within a few decades much of the native population had been destroyed by disease, violence, and a high occurrence of suicide.

As a result, Taíno culture, language, and traditions were generally destroyed, and were claimed to have "vanished" 50 years after Christopher Columbus arrived. Since the early 21st century, efforts have been made to revive and rebuild Taíno culture.

The Roman Catholic Church of chapel, realizing the opportunity to expand its influence, also participated in colonizing the island. On August 8, 1511, Pope Julius II established three dioceses in the New World, one in Puerto Rico and two on the island of Hispaniola under the archbishop of Seville.

The Canon of Salamanca, Alonso Manso, was appointed bishop of the Puerto Rican diocese.

On September 26, 1512, before his arrival on the island, the first school of advanced studies was established by the bishop.

Taking possession in 1513, he became the first bishop to arrive in the Americas. Puerto Rico would also become the first ecclesiastical headquarters in the New World during the reign of Pope Leo X and the general headquarters of the Spanish Inquisition in the New World.

As part of the colonization process, African slaves were brought to the island in 1513. Following the decline of the Taíno population, more slaves were brought to Puerto Rico; however, the number of slaves on the island faded in comparison to those in neighboring islands.

Also, early in the colonization of Puerto Rico, attempts were made to gain control of Puerto Rico from Spain.

The Caribs, a raiding tribe of the Caribbean, attacked Spanish settlements along the banks of the Daguao and Macao rivers in 1514.

They attacked again in 1521 but each time they were disgusted by Spanish firepower. However, these would not be the last attempts at control of Puerto Rico. The European powers quickly realized the potential of the newly discovered lands and attempted to gain control of them.

The first school in Spanish-controlled Puerto Rico was the Escuela de Gramatica, Grammar School. The school was established by Bishop Alonso Manso in 1513, in the area where the Cathedral of San Juan was to be constructed. The school was free of charge and the courses taught were Latin language, literature, history, science, art, philosophy, and theology.

CONTENTS

CHAPTER 1

1493–1898
Beginning of colonization

Puerto Rican have been greatly influenced by its history. With the blend of <u>Taino Indians, Spanish and African cultures</u>, comes a melting pot of people and traditions, as well as the impact of the United States political and social exchange into every aspect of life.

The people of Puerto Rico are known for their warm hospitality. They are often considered very friendly and expressive to strangers...

Puerto Rican culture is rather complex. Some will call it interesting. The culture of this enchanted island is just a series of visual appearances and connections with the environment that make a region and their people different from the rest of the world.

During the early 18 century, the Spaniards to populate the island, took Taino Indians as their spouses.

Later, as labor was needed, the male Indians as well as the females, were placed in different tasks to maintain crops or to build roads...

Then, the African slaves were imported and followed by the introduction of Chinese immigrants. It continued with the coming of Italians, French, German, and even Lebanese people.

Sparked by the possibility of immense wealth, many European powers made attempts to wrest control of the Americas from Spain in the

16th, 17th and 18th centuries. Success in invasion varied, and ultimately all Spanish opponents failed to maintain permanent control of the island.

In 1528, the French, recognizing the strategic value of Puerto Rico, destroyed and burned the southwestern town of San Germán. They also destroyed many of the island's first settlements, including Guánica, Sotomayor, Daguao and Loíza before the local militia forced them to retreat. The only settlement that remained was the capital, San Juan. French corsairs would again sack San Germán in 1538 and 1554.

Spain, determined to defend its possession, began the fortification of the inlet of San Juan in the early 16th century.

In 1532, construction of the first fortifications began with La Fortaleza, 'the Fortress' near the entrance to San Juan Bay.

Seven years later the construction of massive defenses around San Juan began, including Fort San Felipe del Morro astride the entrance to San Juan Bay.

Later, Fort San Cristóbal and Fortín de San Gerónimo built with a financial subsidy from the Mexican mines garrisoned troops and defended against land attacks.

In 1587, engineers Juan de Tejada and Juan Bautista Antonelli redesigned Fort San Felipe del Morro; these changes endure.

Politically, Puerto Rico was reorganized in 1580 into a captaincy general to provide for more autonomy and quick administrative responses to military threats.

Puerto Rico became a colony of the United States in 1898 and many American emigrants came to this wonderful paradise...

Long after Spain had lost control of Puerto Rico, Spanish immigrants continued to arrive to the island. The most significant new immigrant population arrived in the 1960s. This was when thousands of Cubans fled from Fidel Castro's Communist state.

The latest arrivals to Puerto Rico have come from the economically depressed Dominican Republic. This historic mixture of cultures has resulted in a modern Puerto Rico practically without racial problems.

Furthermore, Puerto Rico is full of contrasts. While, Puerto Ricans, love their country and accept the free association with the United States, they also like to emphasize their loyalty not to their culture, but also to their folklore, hospitality, and way of life.

Let just say that the people of Puerto Rico represent a cultural and racial mix...

CHAPTER 2

Christopher Columbus

Columbus was born between 25 August and 31 October 1451 and died 20 May 1506. He was an Italian explorer and navigator who completed four Spanish-based voyages across the Atlantic Ocean sponsored by the Catholic Monarchs of Spain. He opened the way for the widespread European exploration and colonization of the Americas.

His expeditions were the first known European contact with the Caribbean, Central America, and South America.

The name Christopher Columbus is the anglicisation of the Latin Christophorus Columbus. Scholars generally agree that Columbus was born in the Republic of Genoa and spoke a dialect of Ligurian as his first language.

He went to sea at an early age and travelled widely, as far north as the British Isles and as far south as what is now Ghana. He married a Portuguese nobility Filipa Moniz Perestrelo and had his first son Diego. They lived in Lisbon for several years.

Columbus later took a Castilian mistress by the name Beatriz Enríquez de Arana, who had his second son, Fernando.

Self-educated, Columbus was widely read in geography, astronomy, and history. He developed a plan to seek a western sea passage to the East Indies, hoping to profit from the lucrative spice trade.

After the Granada War, and following Columbus's persistent lobbying in multiple kingdoms, the Catholic Monarchs Queen Isabella I and King Ferdinand II agreed to sponsor a journey west.

Columbus left Castile in August 1492 with three ships and made landfall in the Americas on 12 October, ending the period of human habitation in the Americas now referred to as the pre-Columbian era.

His landing place was an island in the Bahamas, known by its native inhabitants as Guanahani. He subsequently visited the islands now known as Cuba and Hispaniola, establishing a colony in what is now Haiti.

Columbus returned to Castile in early 1493, bringing several captured natives with him. Word of his voyage soon spread throughout Europe.

Columbus made three further voyages to the Americas, exploring the Lesser Antilles in 1493, Trinidad and the northern coast of South America in 1498, and the eastern coast of Central America in 1502.

Many of the names he gave to geographical features, particularly islands, are still in use. He also gave the name indies, "Indians", to the indigenous peoples he encountered. The extent to which he was aware that the Americas were a wholly separate landmass is uncertain; he never clearly renounced his belief that he had reached the Far East.

As a colonial governor, Columbus was accused by his contemporaries of significant brutality. He was soon removed from the post as soon as everything came in the open.

Columbus's stressed relationship with the Crown of Castile and its appointed colonial administrators in America that led to his arrest. He was also removed from Hispaniola in 1500.

Later, he prolonged litigation over the perquisites that he and his heirs claimed were owed to them by the crown.

Columbus's expeditions inaugurated a period of exploration, conquest, and colonization that lasted for centuries, thus bringing the Americas into the European sphere of influence.

The transfer of commodities, ideas, and people between the Old World and New World that followed his first voyage are known as the Columbian exchange.

Columbus was widely celebrated in the centuries after his death, but public perception has fractured in the 21st century as scholars have given greater attention to the harms committed under his governance, particularly the beginning of the depopulation of Hispaniola's indigenous.

Taínos caused by mistreatment and Old-World diseases, as well as by that people's enslavement.

Many places in the Western Hemisphere bear his name, including the country of Colombia, the District of Columbia, and British Columbia.

CHAPTER 3

Columbus's birthplace

Christopher Columbus House in Genoa, Italy, an 18th-century reconstruction of the house in which Columbus grew up. The original was likely destroyed during the 1684 bombardment of Genoa.

Columbus's early life is obscure, but scholars believe he was born in the Republic of Genoa between 25 August and 31 October 1451. His father was Domenico Colombo, a wool weaver who worked in Genoa and Savona and who also owned a cheese stand at which young Christopher worked as a helper. His mother was Susanna Fontanarossa.

He had three brothers, Bartolomeo, Giovanni Pellegrino, and Giacomo, also called Diego, as well as a sister named Bianchinetta. His brother Bartolomeo ran a cartography workshop in Lisbon for at least part of his adulthood.

His native language is presumed to have been a Genoese dialect although Columbus probably never wrote in that language. His name in the 16th-century Genoese language was Cristoffa Corombo, Ligurian pronunciation, kriˈʃtɔffa kuˈɹuŋbu. His name in Italian is Cristoforo Colombo, and in Spanish Cristóbal Colón.

In one of his writings, he stated that he went to sea at the age of fourteen.

In 1470, the Colombo family moved to Savona, where Domenico took over a tavern. Some modern authors have argued that he was not from Genoa but, instead, from the Aragon region of Spain or from

Portugal. These competing hypotheses generally have been discounted by mainstream scholars.

In 1473, Columbus began his apprenticeship as business agent for the wealthy Spinola, Centurione, and Di Negro families of Genoa.

Later, he made a trip to Chios, an Aegean Island then ruled by Genoa. In May 1476, he took part in an armed convoy sent by Genoa to carry valuable cargo to northern Europe.

He probably visited Bristol, England, and Galway, Ireland, where he may have visited St. Nicholas Collegiate Church. It has been speculated that he had also gone to Iceland in 1477, although many scholars doubt it.

It is known that in the autumn of 1477, he sailed on a Portuguese ship from Galway to Lisbon, where he found his brother Bartolomeo, and they continued trading for the Centurione family.

CHAPTER 4

Columbus settled in Lisbon
1477 to 1485

In 1478, the Centuriones sent Columbus on a sugar-buying trip to Madeira. He married Felipa Perestrello e Moniz, daughter of Bartolomeu Perestrello, a Portuguese nobleman of Lombard origin, who had been captain of Porto Santo.

In 1479 or 1480, Columbus's son Diego was born. Between 1482 and 1485, Columbus traded along the coasts of West Africa, reaching the Portuguese trading post of Elmina at the Guinea coast, in present-day Ghana.

Before 1484, Columbus returned to Porto Santo to find that his wife had died. He returned to Portugal to settle her estate and take his son Diego with him. He left Portugal for Castile in 1485, where he found a mistress in 1487, a 20-year-old orphan named Beatriz Enríquez de Arana.

It is likely that Beatriz met Columbus when he was in Córdoba, a gathering site of many Genoese merchants and where the court of the Catholic Monarchs was located at intervals.

Beatriz, unmarried at the time, gave birth to Columbus's second son, Fernando Columbus, in July 1488, named for the monarch of Aragon. Columbus recognized the boy as his offspring. Columbus entrusted his older, legitimate son Diego to take care of Beatriz and pay the pension set aside for her following his death, but Diego was negligent in his duties.

Columbus's copy of The Travels of Marco Polo, with his handwritten notes in Latin written on the margins.

Being ambitious, Columbus eventually learned Latin, Portuguese, and Castilian. He read widely about astronomy, geography, and history, including the works of Claudius Ptolemy, Pierre Cardinal d'Ailly's Imago Mundi, the travels of Marco Polo and Sir John Mandeville, Pliny's Natural History, and Pope Pius II's Historia Rerum Ubique Gestarum.

According to historian Edmund Morgan, Columbus was not a scholarly man. Yet he studied these books, made hundreds of marginal notations in them, and came out with ideas about the world that were typically simple and strong and sometimes wrong.

Under the Mongol Empire's hegemony over Asia and the Pax Mongolica, Europeans had long enjoyed a safe land passage on the Silk Road to parts of East Asia, including China and Maritime Southeast Asia, which were sources of valuable goods.

With the fall of Constantinople to the Ottoman Empire in 1453, the Silk Road was closed to Christian traders.

In 1474, the Florentine astronomer Paolo dal Pozzo Toscanelli suggested to King Afonso V of Portugal that sailing west across the Atlantic would be a quicker way to reach the Maluku. Spice Islands, China, and Japan than the route around Africa, but Afonso rejected his proposal.

In the 1480s, Columbus and his brother proposed a plan to reach the East Indies by sailing west. Columbus supposedly wrote Toscanelli in 1481 and received encouragement, along with a copy of a map the astronomer had sent Afonso implying that a westward route to Asia was possible. Columbus's plans were complicated by the opening of the Cape Route to Asia around Africa in 1488.

Carol Delaney and other commentators have argued that Columbus was a Christian that his beliefs motivated his quest for Asia in a variety of ways.

Columbus often wrote about seeking gold in the logbooks of his voyages and wrote about acquiring the precious metal "in such quantity that the sovereigns will undertake and prepare to go conquer the Holy Sepulcher" in a fulfillment of Biblical prophecy.

Columbus also often wrote about converting all races to Christianity. Abbas Hamandi argues that Columbus was motivated by the hope of "delivering Jerusalem from Muslim hands" by "using the resources of newly discovered lands".

Despite a popular misunderstanding to the contrary, all educated Westerners of Columbus's time knew that the Earth is circular, a concept that had been understood since ancient times.

The techniques of cosmic navigation, which uses the position of the Sun and the stars in the sky, had long been in use by astronomers and were beginning to be applied by sailors.

As far back as the third century BC, Eratosthenes had correctly computed the circumference of the Earth by using simple geometry and studying the shadows cast by objects at two remote locations.

In the 1st century BC, Posidonius confirmed Eratosthenes's results by comparing planetary observations at two separate locations. These measurements were widely known among scholars, but Ptolemy's use of the smaller, old-fashioned units of distance led Columbus to underestimate the size of the Earth by about a third.

Three cosmographical parameters determined the bounds of Columbus's enterprise: the distance across the ocean between Europe and Asia, which depended on the extent of the oikumene, i.e., the Eurasian landmass stretching east-west between Spain and China. the

They were the circumference of the Earth and the number of miles or leagues in a degree of longitude, which was possible to deduce from the theory of the relationship between the size of the surfaces of water and the land as held by the followers of Aristotle in medieval times.

From Pierre d'Ailly's Imago Mundi, 1410, Columbus learned of Alfraganus's estimate that a degree of latitude equal to approximately a degree of longitude along the equator spanned 56.67 Arabic miles, equivalent to 66.2 nautical miles, 122.6 kilometers or 76.2 mi, but he did not realize that this was expressed in the Arabic mile, about 1,830 meters or 1.14 mi, rather than the shorter Roman mile, about 1,480 m, with which he was familiar.

Columbus therefore estimated the size of the Earth to be about 75% of Eratosthenes's calculation, and the distance westward from the Canary Islands to the Indies as only 68 degrees, equivalent to 3,080 nmi, 5,700 km: 3,540 mi, a 58% margin of error.

Most scholars of the time accepted Ptolemy's estimate that Eurasia spanned 180° longitude, rather than the actual 130°, to the Chinese mainland, or 150°, to Japan at the latitude of Spain.

Columbus believed an even higher estimate, leaving a smaller percentage for water. In d'Ailly's Imago Mundi, Columbus read Marinus of Tyre's estimate that the longitudinal span of Eurasia was 225° at the latitude of Rhodes.

Some historians, such as Samuel Morison, have suggested that he followed the statement in the apocryphal book 2 Esdras 6:42, that "six parts, of the globe are habitable and the seventh is covered with water."

He was also aware of Marco Polo's claim that Japan, which he called "Cipangu", was some 2,414 km, 1,500 mi, to the east of China "Cathay", and closer to the equator than it is. He was influenced by Toscanelli's idea that there were inhabited islands even farther to the east than Japan, including the mythical Antillia, which he thought might lie not much farther to the west than the Azores.

Based on his sources, Columbus estimated 2,400 mi, 4,400 km; 2,800 mi, from the Canary Islands west to Japan; the actual distance is 10,600 nmi 19,600 km; 12,200 mi.

No ship in the 15th century could have carried enough food and fresh water for such a long voyage, and the dangers involved in navigating through the uncharted ocean would have been formidable.

Most European navigators concluded that a westward voyage from Europe to Asia was unfeasible. The Catholic Monarchs, however, having completed the Reconquista, an expensive war against the Moors in the

Iberian Peninsula, were eager to obtain a competitive edge over other European countries in the quest for trade with the Indies. Columbus's project, though far-fetched, held the promise of such an advantage.

Though Columbus was wrong about the number of degrees of longitude that separated Europe from East Asia and about the distance that each degree represented, he did take advantage of the trade winds, which would prove to be the key to his successful navigation of the Atlantic Ocean. He planned to first sail to the Canary Islands before continuing west with the northeast trade wind.

Part of the return to Spain would require traveling against the wind using an arduous sailing technique called beating, during which progress is made very slowly.

To effectively make the return voyage, Columbus would need to follow the curving trade winds northeastward to the middle latitudes of the North Atlantic, where he would be able to catch the "westerlies" that blow eastward to the coast of Western Europe.

The navigational technique for travel in the Atlantic appears to have been exploited first by the Portuguese, who referred to it as the volta do mar, 'turn of the sea'.

Through his marriage to his first wife, Felipa Perestrello, Columbus had access to the nautical charts and logs that had belonged to her deceased father, Bartolomeu Perestrello, who had served as a captain in the Portuguese navy under Prince Henry the Navigator.

In the mapmaking shop where he worked with his brother Bartolomeo, Columbus also had plenty opportunities to hear the stories of old sailors and about their voyages to the western seas. His knowledge of the Atlantic wind patterns was still imperfect at the time of his first voyage.

By sailing directly west from the Canary Islands during hurricane season, ducking the so-called horse latitudes of the mid-Atlantic, he risked being stranded and running into a tropical cyclone, both of which he avoided by chance.

By about 1484, Columbus proposed his planned voyage to King John II of Portugal. The king submitted Columbus's proposal to his advisors, who rejected it, correctly, on the grounds that Columbus's estimate for a voyage of 2,400 mi was only a quarter of what it should have been.

In 1488, Columbus again appealed to the court of Portugal, and John II again granted him an audience. That meeting also proved unsuccessful, in part because not long afterwards Bartolomeu Dias returned to Portugal with news of his successful rounding of the southern tip of Africa, near the Cape of Good Hope.

Columbus held an interview with the monarchs Ferdinand II of Aragon and Isabella I of Castile, who had united several kingdoms in the Iberian Peninsula by marrying and were now ruling together.

On 1 May 1486, permission having been granted, Columbus presented his plans to Queen Isabella, who, in turn, referred it to a committee. The realized men of Spain, like their counterparts in Portugal, replied that Columbus had clearly underestimated the distance to Asia.

They pronounced the idea impractical and advised the Catholic Monarchs to pass on the proposed project. To keep Columbus from taking his ideas elsewhere, and perhaps to keep their options open, the sovereigns gave him an allowance, totaling about 14,000 maravedis for the year, or about the annual salary of a sailor.

In May 1489, the queen sent him another 10,000 maravedis, and the same year the monarchs furnished him with a letter ordering all cities and towns under their dominion to provide him food and lodging at no cost.

Columbus also dispatched his brother Bartolomeo to the court of Henry VII of England to inquire whether the English crown might sponsor his expedition, but he was captured by pirates en route, and only arrived in early 1491.

By that time, Columbus had retreated to <u>La Rábida Friary</u>, where the Spanish crown sent him 20,000 maravedis to buy new clothes and instructions to return to the Spanish court for renewed discussions.

Columbus waited at King Ferdinand's camp until Ferdinand and Isabella conquered Granada, the last Muslim stronghold on the Iberian Peninsula, in January 1492.

A council led by Isabella's confessor, Hernando de Talavera, found Columbus's proposal to reach the Indies implausible. Columbus had left for France when Ferdinand intervened, first sending Talavera and Bishop Diego Deza to appeal to the queen.

The king's clerk Luis finally convinced Isabella de Santángel, who argued that Columbus would take his ideas elsewhere, and offered to help arrange the funding. Isabella then sent a royal guard to get Columbus, who had traveled over 10 km, toward Córdoba.

In the April 1492 "Capitulations of Santa Fe", King Ferdinand and Queen Isabella promised Columbus that if he succeeded, he would be given the rank of Admiral of the Ocean Sea and appointed Viceroy and Governor of all the new lands he might claim for Spain.

He had the right to nominate three persons, from whom the sovereigns would choose one, for any office in the new lands. He would be entitled to 10%, diezmo, of all the revenues from the new lands in perpetuity. He also would have the option of buying one-eighth interest in any commercial venture in the new lands and receive one-eighth, ochavo, of the profits.

In 1500, during his third voyage to the Americas, Columbus was arrested and dismissed from his posts. He and his sons, Diego, and Fernando, then conducted a lengthy series of court cases against the Castilian crown, known as the pleitos colombinos, alleging that the Crown had illegally revoked on its contractual obligations to Columbus and his heirs.

The Columbus family had some success in their first litigation, as a judgment of 1511 confirmed Diego's position as viceroy but reduced his powers. Diego resumed litigation in 1512, which lasted until 1536, and further disputes initiated by heirs continued until 1790.

Between 1492 and 1504, Columbus completed four round-trip voyages between Spain and the Americas, each voyage being sponsored by the Crown of Castile.

On his first voyage he reached the Americas, initiating the European exploration and colonization of the continent, as well as the Columbian exchange. His role in history is thus important to the Age of Discovery, Western history, and human history temporary restraining order large.

In Columbus's letter on the first voyage, published following his first return to Spain, he claimed that he had reached Asia, as previously described by Marco Polo and other Europeans.

Over his subsequent voyages, Columbus refused to acknowledge that the lands he visited and claimed for Spain were not part of Asia, in the face of mounting evidence to the contrary.

This might explain, in part, why the American continent was named after the Florentine explorer <u>Amerigo Vespucci</u>, who received credit for recognizing it as a <u>"New World"</u>, and not after Columbus.

CHAPTER 5

Facts About Christopher Columbus

Although Columbus remains a leading historical figure around the world and has been researched and written about for centuries, there are many details of his life that are still a mystery.

Many scholars agree that he was born in Genoa, which is now part of Italy, although there are theories that he may have originated in Spain or even in Poland or Greece.

In Italian he is known as Cristoforo Colombo, which was long thought to be his birth name, and in Spanish as Cristóbal Colón. He has also been referred to as Christoual, Christovam, Christofferus de Colombo, and even Xpoual de Colón. There is even a theory that he adopted the name from a pirate named Colombo.

Columbus's boats names are also in question. If you ask any American schoolchild and they'll tell you Columbus's ships were named Niña, Pinta, and Santa Maria. However, at least two of those were nicknames.

In Columbus's time it was the custom in Spain to name ships after saints and to call them by nicknames instead. La Niña was likely a nickname for a ship called Santa Clara. The nickname is thought to have come from the name of the ship's owner, Juan Niño. It is unknown what the Pinta's original name might have been. Santa Maria is a perfectly saintly name for the third, which was also nicknamed La Gallega.

He made four journeys to the "New World". In 1492 Columbus did sail the ocean blue. He also sailed it in 1493, 1498, and 1502. Although many people may have an image of Columbus planting a flag in the lower half of Florida, he only explored a small area of the Caribbean, which included the Bahamas, Cuba, and Jamaica, and parts of Central America.

Columbus remains did about as much traveling as he did in life. After he died in 1506, he was buried in Valladolid, Spain. Three years later his remains were taken to his family mausoleum, which was in Sevilla. In 1542, in accordance with the will of his son Diego, Columbus's remains were transferred to Santo Domingo, Hispaniola, now in the Dominican Republic.

Hispaniola was ceded to France by Spain, and in 1795 Columbus's bones were moved to Havana, Cuba. More than a hundred years later they were shipped back across the Atlantic and returned to Sevilla in 1898.

At the time Columbus made his famous journey, a lot of overseas travel was guesswork. The exact size of the planet Earth was unknown, and there were two main ways of measuring degrees of latitude, the method developed by the Greek philosopher Poseidonius and the method developed by the medieval Arabs.

In making his own calculations, Columbus argued that the circumference yielded by both methods was the same ignoring, or forgetting, that Arab miles were longer than Roman miles.

Using that data, which rendered the planet about 25 percent smaller, Columbus assured his backers that his small wooden ships could make it from Spain to Japan in 30 days. Some scholars think Columbus willfully misrepresented the distance, but the jury is still out.

CHAPTER 6

First voyage 1492–1493

On the evening of August 3, 1492, Columbus departed from Palos de la Frontera with three ships. The largest was a carrack, the Santa María, owned and captained by Juan de la Cosa, and under Columbus's direct command. The other two were smaller caravels, the Pinta and the Niña, piloted by the Pinzón brothers.

Columbus first sailed to the Canary Islands. There he restocked provisions and made repairs then departed from San Sebastián de La Gomera on 6 September, for what turned out to be a five-week voyage across the ocean.

On October 7, the crew spotted "immense flocks of birds". On 11 October 11, Columbus changed the fleet's course to due west, and sailed through the night, believing land was soon to be found.

At about 02:00 the following morning, a lookout on the Pinta, Rodrigo de Triana, spotted land. The captain of the Pinta, Martín Alonso Pinzón, verified the sight of land and alerted Columbus.

Columbus later maintained that he had already seen a light on the land a few hours earlier, thereby claiming for himself the lifetime pension promised by Ferdinand and Isabella to the first person to sight land. Columbus called this island, in what is now the Bahamas, San Salvador meaning "Holy Savior"; the natives called it Guanahani. Christopher Columbus's journal entry of October 12, 1492, stated:

"I saw some who had marks of wounds on their bodies, and I made signs to them asking what they were; and they showed me how people from other islands nearby came there and tried to take them, and how they defended themselves; and I believed and believe that they come here from tierra firme to take them captive.

They should be good and intelligent servants, for I see that they say very quickly everything that is said to them; and I believe they would become Christians very easily, for it seemed to me that they had no religion. Our Lord pleasing, at the time of my departure I will take six of them from here to Your Highnesses in order that they may learn to speak".

Columbus called the inhabitants of the lands that he visited Los Indios, Spanish for "Indians". He initially encountered the Lucayan, Taíno, and Arawak peoples.

Noting their gold ear ornaments, Columbus took some of the Arawaks prisoner and insisted that they guide him to the source of the gold. Columbus did not believe he needed to create a fortified outpost, writing, "the people here are simple in war-like matters. I could conquer the whole of them with fifty men and govern them as I pleased."

The Taínos told Columbus that another Indigenous tribe, Caribs, were fierce warriors and cannibals, who made frequent raids on the Taínos, often capturing their women.

Columbus also explored the northeast coast of Cuba, where he landed on October 28. On the night of November 26, Martín Alonso Pinzón took the Pinta on an unauthorized expedition in search of an island called "Babeque" or "Baneque", which the natives had told him was rich in gold. Columbus, for his part, continued to the northern coast of Hispaniola, where he landed on December 6.

There, the Santa María ran aground on December 25, 1492 and had to be abandoned. The wreck was used as a target for cannon fire to impress the native peoples.

Columbus was received by the native cacique Guacanagari, who gave him permission to leave some of his men behind. Columbus left 39 men, including the interpreter Luis de Torres, and founded the settlement of La Navidad, in present-day Haiti.

Columbus took more natives prisoner and continued his exploration. He kept sailing along the northern coast of Hispaniola with a single ship until he encountered Pinzón and the Pinta on January 6.

On January 13, 1493, Columbus made his last stop of this voyage in the Americas, in the Bay of Rincón in northeast Hispaniola. There he encountered the Ciguayos, the only natives who offered violent resistance during this voyage.

The Ciguayos refused to trade the number of bows and arrows that Columbus desired; in the ensuing clash one Ciguayo was stabbed in the buttocks and another wounded with an arrow in his chest.

Due of these events, Columbus called the inlet the Golfo de Las Flechas, Bay of Arrows.

Columbus headed for Spain on the Niña, but a storm separated him from the Pinta, and forced the Niña to stop at the island of Santa Maria in the Azores.

Half of his crew went ashore to say prayers of thanksgiving in a chapel for having survived the storm. While praying, they were imprisoned by the governor of the island, apparently on suspicion of being pirates.

After a two-day confrontation, the prisoners were released, and Columbus again set sail for Spain.

Another storm forced Columbus into the port at Lisbon. From there he went to Vale do Paraíso north of Lisbon to meet King John II of Portugal, who told Columbus that he believed the voyage to be in violation of the 1479 Treaty of Alcáçovas.

After spending more than a week in Portugal, Columbus set sail towards Spain. He returned to Palos on March 15, 1493. He was given a hero's welcome and soon afterward received by Isabella and Ferdinand in Barcelona.

Columbus's letter on the first voyage, dispatched to the Spanish court, was instrumental in spreading the news throughout Europe about his voyage. Almost immediately after his arrival in Spain, printed versions began to appear, and word of his voyage spread rapidly.

Most people initially believed that he had reached Asia. The Bulls of Donation, three papal bulls of Pope Alexander VI delivered in 1493, claimed to grant overseas territories to Portugal and the Catholic Monarchs of Spain. They were replaced by the Treaty of Tordesillas of 1494.

The two earliest published copies of Columbus's letter on the first voyage aboard the Niña were donated in 2017 by the Jay I. Kislak Foundation to the University of Miami library in Coral Gables, Florida, where they are kept.

CHAPTER 7

Second Voyage 1493–1496

On September 24, 1493, Columbus sailed from Cádiz with 17 ships, and supplies to establish permanent colonies in the Americas. He sailed with nearly 1,500 men, including sailors, soldiers, priests, carpenters, stonemasons, metalworkers, and farmers.

Among the expedition members were Alvarez Chanca, a physician who wrote a detailed account of the second voyage; Juan Ponce de León, the first governor of Puerto Rico and Florida; the father of Bartolomé de las Casas; Juan de la Cosa, a cartographer who is credited with making the first world map portraying the New World; and Columbus's youngest brother Diego.

The fleet stopped at the Canary Islands to take on more supplies, and set sail again on October 7, deliberately taking a more southern course than on the first voyage.

On November 3, they arrived in the Windward Islands; the first island they encountered was named <u>Dominica</u> by Columbus, but not finding a good harbor there, they anchored off a nearby smaller island, which he named <u>Mariagalante</u>, now a part of Guadeloupe and called <u>Marie-Galante</u>.

Other islands named by Columbus on this voyage were Montserrat, Antigua, Saint Martin, the Virgin Islands, as well as many others.

On November 22, Columbus returned to Hispaniola to visit La Navidad, where 39 Spaniards had been left during the first voyage.

Columbus found the fort in ruins, destroyed by the Taínos after some of the Spaniards reportedly provoked their hosts with their unrestrained lust for gold and women.

Then Columbus established a poorly located and short-lived settlement to the east, La Isabela, in the present-day Dominican Republic.

From April to August 1494, Columbus explored Cuba and Jamaica, then returned to Hispaniola. By the end of 1494, disease and famine had killed two-thirds of the Spanish settlers.

Columbus implemented encomienda, a Spanish labor system that rewarded conquerors with the labor of conquered non-Christian people. Columbus executed Spanish colonists for minor crimes and used dismemberment as punishment.

Columbus and the colonists enslaved the indigenous people, including children. Natives were beaten, raped, and tortured for the location of imagined gold. Thousands committed suicide rather than face the oppression.

In February 1495, Columbus rounded up about 1,500 Arawaks, some of whom had rebelled, in a great slave raid. About 500 of the strongest were shipped to Spain as slaves, with about two hundred of those dying en route.

In June 1495, the Spanish crown sent ships and supplies to Hispaniola. In October, Florentine merchant Gianotto Berardi, who had won the contract to provision the fleet of Columbus's second voyage and to supply the colony on Hispaniola, received almost 40,000 maravedís worth of enslaved Indians.

Berardi renewed his effort to get supplies to Columbus and was working to organize a fleet when he suddenly died in December.

On March 10, 1496, having been away about 30 months, the fleet departed La Isabela. On June 8, the crew spotted land somewhere between Lisbon and Cape St. Vincent and disembarked in Cádiz on June 11.

CHAPTER 8

Third voyage

On May 30, 1498, Columbus left with six ships from Sanlúcar, Spain. The fleet called at Madeira and the Canary Islands, where it divided in two, with three ships heading for Hispaniola and the other three vessels, commanded by Columbus, sailing south to the Cape Verde Islands and then westward across the Atlantic.

It is probable that this expedition was intended at least partly to confirm rumors of a large continent south of the Caribbean Sea, that is, South America.

On July 31, they spotted Trinidad, the most southerly of the Caribbean islands.

On August 5, Columbus sent several small boats ashore on the southern side of the Paria Peninsula in what is now Venezuela, near the mouth of the Orinoco River.

This was the first recorded landing of Europeans on the mainland of South America, which Columbus realized must be a continent.

The fleet then sailed to the islands of Chacachacare and Margarita, reaching the latter on August 14, and saw Tobago and Grenada from afar, according to some scholars.

On August 19, Columbus returned to Hispaniola. There he found settlers in rebellion against his rule, and his unfulfilled promises of riches. Columbus had some of the Europeans tried for their disobedience; at least one rebel leader was hanged.

In October 1499, Columbus sent two ships to Spain, asking the Court of Spain to appoint a royal commissioner to help him govern.

By this time, accusations of tyranny and incompetence on the part of Columbus had also reached the Court. The sovereigns sent Francisco de Bobadilla, a relative of Marquesa Beatriz de Bobadilla, a patron of Columbus and a close friend of Queen Isabella, to investigate the accusations of brutality made against the Admiral.

Reaching in Santo Domingo while Columbus was away, Bobadilla was immediately met with complaints about all three Columbus brothers. He moved into Columbus's house and seized his property, took depositions from the Admiral's enemies, and declared himself governor.

Bobadilla reported to Spain that Columbus once punished a man that was found guilty of stealing corn by having his ears and nose cut off and then selling him into slavery. He claimed that Columbus regularly used torture and mutilation to govern Hispaniola.

Testimony recorded in the report stated that Columbus congratulated his brother Bartolomeo on "defending the family" when the latter ordered a woman paraded naked through the streets and then had her tongue cut because she had "spoken ill of the admiral and his brothers".

The document also describes how Columbus put down native unrest and revolt: he first ordered a brutal suppression of the uprising in which many natives were killed, and then paraded their dismembered bodies through the streets to discourage further rebellion. Columbus strongly denied the charges.

The objectivity and accuracy of the accusations and investigations of Bobadilla toward Columbus and his brothers have been disputed by historians, given the anti-Italian sentiment of the Spaniards and Bobadilla's desire to take over Columbus's position.

In early October 1500, Columbus and Diego presented themselves to Bobadilla, and were put in chains aboard La Gorda, the ship on which Bobadilla had arrived the island of Santo Domingo.

They were returned to Spain and were put in jail for six weeks before King Ferdinand ordered their release. Not long after, the king and queen summoned the Columbus brothers to the Alhambra palace in Granada.

The rulers expressed anger at Bobadilla's actions, who was then recalled and ordered to make repayments of the property he had confiscated from Columbus.

The royal couple heard the brothers' pleas; restored their freedom and wealth; and, after much persuasion, agreed to fund Columbus's fourth voyage.

Nicolás de Ovando was to replace Bobadilla and be the new governor of the West Indies.

New light was dropped on the arrest of Columbus and his brother Bartolomeo, the Adelantado, with the discovery by archivist Isabel Aguirre of an incomplete copy of the testimonies against them gathered by Francisco de Bobadilla in Santo Domingo in 1500.

She found a manuscript copy of this inquiry in the Archive of Simancas, Spain, uncatalogued until she and Consuelo Varela published their book, La caída de Cristóbal Colón: el juicio de Bobadilla, The fall of Christopher Colón: the judgement of Bobadilla, in 2006.

CHAPTER 9

Fourth voyage

On May 9, 1502, Columbus left Cádiz with his flagship Santa María and three other vessels. The ships were crewed by 140 men, including his brother Bartolomeo as second in command and his son Fernando.

He sailed to Arzila on the Moroccan coast to rescue Portuguese soldiers who were besieged by the Moors. The siege had been lifted by the time they arrived, so the Spaniards stay only a day and continued to the Canary Islands.

The fourth voyage was final years of Christopher Columbus. The winter and spring of 1501–02 were exceedingly busy. The four chosen ships were bought, fitted, and crewed, and some 20 of Columbus's extant letters and memoranda were written then, many in pardon of Bobadilla's charges, others pressing even harder the nearness of the Earthly Paradise and the need to reconquer Jerusalem.

Columbus took to calling himself "Christbearer" in his letters and to using a strange and mystical signature, never satisfactorily explained. He began also, with all these thoughts and pressures in mind, to compile his Book of Privileges, which defended the titles and financial claims of the Columbus family, and his apocalyptic Book of Prophecies, which includes several biblical passages.

The first collection seems an odd companion to the second, yet both were closely linked in the admiral's own mind. He seems to have been certain that his mission was divinely guided. Thus, the arrogance of his spiritual aspirations increased as the threats to his personal ones mounted.

During all these efforts and hazards, Columbus sailed from Cádiz on his fourth voyage on May 9, 1502.

Columbus's kings had lost much of their confidence in him, and there is much to suggest that pity mingled with hope in their support. His four ships contrasted sharply with the 30 granted to the governor Ovando.

His illnesses were worsening, and the hostility to his rule in Hispaniola was relentless. Thus, Ferdinand and Isabella forbade him to return there. He was to resume, instead, his interrupted exploration of the "other world" to the south that he had found on his third voyage and to look particularly for gold and the passage to India.

Columbus expected to meet the Portuguese navigator Vasco da Gama in the East, and the rulers instructed him on the appropriate courteous behavior for such a meeting.

Another sign was perhaps, that they did not entirely trust him. They were right. He departed from Gran Canaria on the night of May 25, 1502, made landfall in Martinique on June 15, 1502, after the fastest crossing to date, and was, by June 29, 1502, demanding entrance to Santo Domingo on Hispaniola. Only on being refused entry by Ovando did he sail away to the west and south.

From July to September 1502, he explored the coast of Jamaica, the southern shore of Cuba, Honduras, and the Mosquito Coast of Nicaragua.

Columbus act of Caribbean trans navigation, which took him to Bonacca Island off Cape Honduras on July 30, deserves to be reckoned on a par, as to difficulty, with that of crossing the Atlantic, and the admiral was justly proud of it.

The fleet continued southward along Costa Rica. Constantly probing for the passage, Columbus sailed round the Chiriquí Lagoon, in Panama, in October.

Then, searching for gold, he explored the Panamanian region of Veragua in the foulest of weather.

To exploit the promising gold yield, he was beginning to find there, the admiral in February 1503 attempted to establish a trading post at Santa María de Belén on the bank of the Belén, Bethlehem, River under the command of Bartholomew Columbus.

However, Indigenous resistance and the poor condition of his ships, of which only two remained, fearfully holed by shipworm, caused him to turn back to Hispaniola.

On this voyage disaster again struck. Against Columbus's better judgment, his pilots turned the fleet north too soon. The ships could not make the distance and had to be stranded on the coast of Jamaica. By June 1503 Columbus and his crews were castaways.

Columbus had hoped, as he said to his sovereigns, that "my hard and troublesome voyage may yet turn out to be my noblest"; it was in fact the most disappointing of all and the unluckiest. In its explorations the fleet had missed discovering the Pacific, across the isthmus of Panama, and failed to contact the Maya of Yucatán by the narrowest of margins.

Two of the men, Diego Méndez and Bartolomeo Fieschi, captains of the wrecked ships La Capitana and Vizcaíno, respectively. They left about July 17 by canoe to get help for the castaways; although they managed to traverse the 450 miles,720 km, of open sea to Hispaniola, Ovando made no great haste to deliver that help.

In the meantime, the admiral displayed his judgement once again by correctly predicting an eclipse of the Moon from his astronomical tables, thus frightening the local peoples into providing food; but rescuers did not arrive until June 1504.

Columbus and his men did not reach Hispaniola until August 13 of that year. On November 7 he went back to Sanlúcar and found that Queen Isabella, his main supporter, had made her will and was dying.

Columbus always claimed that he had found the true Indies and Cathay in the face of mounting evidence that he had not. Perhaps he genuinely believed that he had been there; in any event, his disallowances of the "New World" hindered his goals of nobility and wealth and dented his later reputation.

Columbus had been distant from his companions and intending colonists, and he had been a poor judge of the ambitions, and perhaps the failings, of those who sailed with him. This combination proved damaging to almost all his hopes.

Nonetheless, it would be wrong to suppose that Columbus spent his final two years completely in illness, poverty, and forgetfulness. His son Diego was well established at court, and the admiral himself lived in Sevilla in some style.

His "tenth" of the gold diggings in Hispaniola, guaranteed in 1493, provided a substantial revenue, against which his Genoese bankers allowed him to draw, and one of the few ships to escape a hurricane off Hispaniola in 1502, in which Bobadilla himself went down, was that carrying Columbus's gold.

He felt himself ill-used and shortchanged nonetheless, and these years were stained, for both him and King Ferdinand, by his constant pressing for redress.

Columbus followed the court from Segovia to Salamanca and Valladolid, attempting to gain an audience. He knew that his life was close to its end, and in August 1505 he began to amend his will. He died on May 20, 1506.

First, he was laid in the Franciscan friary in Valladolid, then taken to the family tomb established at the Carthusian monastery of Las Cuevas in Sevilla.

In 1542, by the will of his son Diego, Columbus's bones were laid with his own in the Cathedral of Santo Domingo, Hispaniola. now in the Dominican Republic.

After Spain surrendered Hispaniola to France, the remains were moved to Havana, Cuba, in 1795 and returned to Sevilla in 1898.

In 1877, however, workers at the cathedral in Santo Domingo claimed to have found another set of bones that were marked as those of Columbus. Since 1992 these bones have been buried in the Columbus Lighthouse, Faro de Colón.

CHAPTER 10

Christopher Columbus's Travels

There are few materials remains of Columbus's travels. Efforts to find the Spaniards' first settlement on Hispaniola have so far failed.

The present-day fishing village of Bord de Mer de Lemonade, near Cap-Haïtien, Haiti, may be close to the original site.

A Taino chieftain's settlement has been identified nearby. Concepción de la Vega, which Columbus founded on the second voyage, may be the present La Vega Viera, in the Dominican Republic.

Excavations at the site of La Isabela were still ongoing in the early 21st century. At Sevilla la Nueva, Jamaica, is where Columbus's two ships were stranded on the fourth voyage.

The techniques of skeletal paleopathology and paleo demography were applied with some success to determine the fates of the native populations.

Most of the surviving primary sources about Columbus are not private diaries or missives; instead, they were intended to be read by other people. There is an element of manipulation about them. There is a fact that must be carried fully in mind for their proper understanding.

Foremost among these sources are the journals written by Columbus himself for his ruler.

One for the first voyage, now lost though partly reconstructed; one for the second, almost wholly gone; and one for the third, which, like the first, is accessible through reconstructions made by using later quotations.

Each of the journals may be supplemented by letters and reports to and from the sovereigns and their trusted officials and friends, provisioning decrees from the rulers, and, in the case of the second voyage, letters and reports of letters from fellow voyagers, especially Michele da Cuneo, Diego Alvarez Chanca, and Guillermo Coma.

There is no journal and only one letter from the fourth voyage, but a complete roster and payroll survive from this, alone of all the voyages.

In addition, an eyewitness account survived that has been plausibly attributed to Columbus's younger son, Ferdinand. Ferdinand traveled with his father.

Further light is thrown upon the explorations by the so-called Pleitos de Colón, judicial documents concerning Columbus's disputed legacy. A more recent discovery is a copybook that supposedly contains five narrative letters and two personal ones from Columbus. All previously unknown, as well as additional copies of two known letters. All those letters claimed as authentic.

Supplemental narratives included The Life of the Admiral Christopher Columbus, which has been attributed to Ferdinand Columbus.

La Historia de los Reyes Católicos, c. 1500 of Andrés Bernáldez, a friend of Columbus and chaplain to the archbishop of Sevilla, and the Historia de las Indias, which was compiled about 1550–63 by Bartolomé de Las Casas, former bishop of Chiapas and a champion of the indigenous people of the Americas.

Columbus's intentions and presuppositions may be better understood by examining the few books still surviving from his own library. Some of these were extensively annotated, often by the admiral and sometimes by his brother Bartholomew, including copies of the Imago mundi by the 15th-century French theologian Pierre d'Ailly.

He had probably already read and annotated at three texts before he set out on his first voyage to the "Indies." Columbus was a deeply religious and reflective man as well as a distinguished seaman, and being largely self-taught, he had a reverence for learning, perhaps especially the learning of his most influential Spanish supporters.

A striking manifestation of his sensibilities is the Book of Prophecies, a collection of pronouncements largely taken from the Bible and seeming to bear directly on his role in the western voyages; the book was probably compiled by Columbus and his friend the Carthusian friar Gorricio between September 1501 and March 1502, with additions until approximately 1505.

CHAPTER 11

Wrong Calculations

C ontrary to common tradition, Columbus's generations never thought that the world was flat. Educated Europeans had known that the Earth was circular in shape since at least the early 7th century when the popular Etymologies of St. Isidore of Sevilla were produced in Spain.

Columbus's miscalculations, such as they were, lay in other areas. First, his estimate of the sea distance to be crossed to Cathay was wildly inaccurate.

Columbus rejected Ptolemy's estimate of the journey from West to East overland, substituting a far longer one based on a chart, now lost, supplied by the Florentine mathematician and geographer Paolo Toscanelli, and on Columbus's preference for the calculations of the Classical geographer Marinus of Tyre.

In addition, Columbus's reading primarily of the 13th–14th-century Venetian Marco Polo's Travels gave him the idea that the lands of the East stretched out far around the back of the globe, with the island of Cipango, itself surrounded by islands, located a further 1,500 miles, 2,400 km, from the mainland of Cathay.

He seems to have argued that this archipelago might be near the Azores. Columbus also read the prophet Salathiel-Ezra in the books of Esdras, from the Apocrypha, especially 2 Esdras 6:42, in which the prophet states that the Earth is six parts land to one of water, thus reinforcing these ideas of the proportion of land- to sea-crossing.

The mistake was further compounded by his peculiar view of the length of a degree of geographic latitude. The degree, according to Arabic calculators, consisted of 562/3 Arab miles, and an Arab mile measured 6,481 feet. Given that a nautical mile measures 6,076 feet, 1,852 m., meters this degree amounts to approximately 60.45 nautical miles.

Columbus, however, used the Italian mile of 4,847 feet, 1,477.5 metres, for his computations and thus arrived at approximately 45 nautical miles, 83 km, to a degree.

This shortened the supposed distance across the sea westward to such an extent that Zaiton, Marco Polo's great port of Cathay, would have lain a little to the east of present-day San Diego, California, U.S.

Also, the islands of Cipango would have been about as far north of the Equator as the Virgin Islands, close to where Columbus made his landfalls.

The miscalculation of distance may have been willful on Columbus's part and made with an eye to his sponsors. The first journal suggests that Columbus may have been aware of his inaccuracy, for he consistently concealed from his sailors the great number of miles they had covered, lest they become fearful for the journey back.

Such manipulations may be interpreted as evidence of bravery and the need to inspire confidence rather than of simple dishonesty or error.

CHAPTER 12

Illness, and death

Columbus had always claimed that the conversion of non-believers was one reason for his explorations, and he grew increasingly religious in his later years.

Probably with the assistance of his son Diego and his friend the Carthusian monk Gaspar Gorricio, Columbus produced two books during his later years: a Book of Privileges, 1502, detailing and documenting the rewards from the Spanish Crown to which he believed he and his heirs were entitled, and a Book of Prophecies, 1505, in which passages from the Bible were used to place his achievements as an explorer in the context of Christian eschatology.

In his later years, Columbus demanded that the Crown of Castile give him his tenth of all the riches and trade goods yielded by the new lands, as stipulated in the <u>Capitulations of Santa Fe</u>.

Because he had been relieved of his duties as governor, the Crown did not feel bound by that contract and his demands were rejected. After his death, his heirs sued the Crown for a part of the profits from trade with America, as well as other rewards. This led to a protracted series of legal disputes known as the <u>pleitos colombinos, "Columbian lawsuits"</u>.

During a violent storm on his first return voyage, Columbus, then 41, had suffered an attack of what was believed at the time to be urarthritis.

In subsequent years, he was plagued with what was thought to be influenza and other fevers, bleeding from the eyes, temporary blindness, and prolonged attacks of gout.

The occurrences increased in duration and severity, sometimes leaving Columbus bedridden for months at a time, and culminated in his death 14 years later.

Based on Columbus's lifestyle and the described symptoms, some modern commentators suspect that he suffered from reactive arthritis, rather than gouty arthritis.

Reactive arthritis is a joint inflammation caused by intestinal bacterial infections or after acquiring certain sexually transmitted diseases, primarily chlamydia or gonorrhea.

In 2006, Frank C. Arnett, a medical doctor, and historian Charles Merrill, published their paper in The American Journal of the Medical Sciences proposing that Columbus had a form of reactive arthritis.

Merrill made the case in that same paper that Columbus was the son of Catalans and his mother possibly a member of a prominent converso, converted Jew, family.

"It seems likely that Columbus acquired reactive arthritis from food poisoning on one of his ocean voyages because of poor sanitation and improper food preparation," says Arnett, a rheumatologist and professor of internal medicine, pathology, and laboratory medicine at the University of Texas Medical School at Houston.

Some historians such as H. Michael Tarver and Emily Slape, as well as medical doctors such as Arnett and Antonio Rodríguez Cuartero, believe that Columbus had such a form of reactive arthritis, but according to other authorities, this is "speculative", or "very speculative".

After his arrival to Sanlúcar from his fourth voyage and Queen Isabella's death, an ill Columbus settled in Seville in April 1505.

He stubbornly continued to make pleas to the Crown to defend his own personal privileges and his family's. He moved to Segovia, where the court was at the time, on a graze by early 1506.

On the wedding of King Ferdinand with Germaine of Foix in Valladolid, Spain, in March 1506, Columbus moved to that city to persist with his demands.

On 20 May 1506, aged 54, Columbus died in Valladolid.

CHAPTER 13

The Tomb in Seville Cathedral

Columbus remains were carried by kings of Castile, Leon, Aragon, and Navarre. A large white, black, and gold tomb elaborately adorned with sculpture and writing, claiming to be the resting place of Cristobal Colon.

Tomb in Columbus Lighthouse, <u>Santo Domingo Este</u>, Dominican Republic

Columbus's remains were first buried at a convent in Valladolid, then moved to the monastery of La Cartuja in Seville, southern Spain, by the will of his son Diego.

They may have been exhumed in 1513 and buried at the Seville Cathedral. In about 1536, the remains of both Columbus and his son Diego were moved to a cathedral in Colonial Santo Domingo, in the present-day Dominican Republic; Columbus had requested to be buried on the island.

By some accounts, in 1793, when France took over the entire island of Hispaniola, Columbus's remains were moved to Havana, Cuba.

Cuba became independent following the Spanish American War in 1898, at least some of these remains were moved back to the Seville Cathedral, where they were placed on an elaborate catafalque.

In June 2003, DNA samples were taken from these remains as well as those of Columbus's brother Diego and younger son Fernando.

Initial observations suggested that the bones did not appear to match Columbus's figure or age at death.

DNA extraction proved difficult; only short fragments of mitochondrial DNA could be isolated. These matched corresponding DNA from Columbus's brother, supporting that both individuals had shared the same mother.

Such evidence, together with anthropologic and historic analyses, led the researchers to conclude that the remains belonged to Christopher Columbus.

In 1877, a priest discovered a lead box at Santo Domingo inscribed: "Discoverer of America, First Admiral". Inscriptions found the next year read "Last of the remains of the first admiral, Sire Christopher Columbus, discoverer."

The box contained bones of an arm and a leg, as well as a bullet. These remains were considered legitimate by physician and U.S. Assistant Secretary of State John Eugene Osborne, who suggested in 1913 that they travel through the Panama Canal as a part of its opening ceremony.

Those remains were kept at the Basilica Cathedral of Santa María la Menor, in the Colonial City of Santo Domingo, before being moved to the Columbus Lighthouse, Santo Domingo Este, inaugurated in 1992.

The authorities in Santo Domingo have never allowed these remains to be DNA-tested, so it is unconfirmed whether they are from Columbus's body as well.

CHAPTER 14

The Legacy

The voyages of Columbus are considered a turning point in human history, marking the beginning of globalization, and accompanying demographic, commercial, economic, social, and political changes.

His explorations resulted in permanent contact between the two hemispheres, and the term "pre-Columbian" is used to refer to the cultures of the Americas before the arrival of Columbus and his European successors.

The resulting Columbian exchange saw the massive exchange of animals, plants, fungi, diseases, technologies, mineral wealth, and ideas.

In the first century after his activities, Columbus's figure largely suffered in the backwaters of history, and his reputation was affected by his failures as a colonial administrator.

His legacy was somewhat rescued from forgetfulness when he began to appear as a character in Italian and Spanish plays and poems from the late 16th century onward.

Columbus was subsumed into the Western narrative of colonization and empire building, which invoked notions of translation to underline who was considered "civilized" and who was not.

His explorations resulted in permanent contact between the two hemispheres, and the term "pre-Columbian" is used to refer to the cultures of the Americas before the arrival of Columbus and his European successors.

The succeeding Columbian exchange saw the massive exchange of animals, plants, fungi, diseases, technologies, mineral wealth, and ideas.

The Americanization of the figure of Columbus began in later decades of the 18th century, after the revolutionary period of the United States, elevating the status of his reputation to a national myth, homo americanus.

His landing became a powerful icon as an "image of American genesis".

The Discovery of America sculpture, showing Columbus and a cowering Indian maiden, was commissioned on 3 April 1837, when U.S. President Martin Van Buren sanctioned the engineering of Luigi Persico's design.

This representation of Columbus's triumph and the Indian's started demonstrations of white superiority over savage, naive Indians.

As recorded during its unveiling in 1844, the sculpture extends to "represent the meeting of the two races", as Persico captures their first interaction, highlighting the "moral and intellectual inferiority" of Indians. Placed outside the U.S. Capitol building where it remained until its removal in the mid-20th century, the sculpture reflected the contemporary view of whites in the U.S. toward the Natives; they are labeled "merciless Indian savages" in the United States Declaration of Independence.

In 1836, Pennsylvania senator and future U.S. President James Buchanan, who proposed the sculpture, described it as representing "the great discoverer when he first bounded with ecstasy upon the shore, ail his works past, presenting a hemisphere to the astonished world, with the name America inscribed upon it.

At the same time as he is thus standing upon the shore, a female savage, with wonder portrayed in her countenance, is gazing upon him."

The American Columbus myth was reconfigured later in the century when he was enlisted as an ethnic hero by immigrants to the United States who were not of Anglo-Saxon stock, such as Jewish, Italian, and Irish people, who claimed Columbus as a sort of ethnic founding father.

Catholics unsuccessfully tried to promote him for canonization in the 19th century.

From the 1990s onward, a narrative of Columbus being responsible for the killing of indigenous peoples and environmental destruction began to compete with the then predominant discourse of Columbus as Christ-bearer, scientist, or father of America.

Those narrative featured the negative effects of Columbus' conquests on native populations. Exposed to Old World diseases, the indigenous populations of the New World collapsed, and were largely replaced by Europeans and Africans, who brought with them new methods of farming, business, power, and religious worship.

Though Christopher Columbus came to be considered the European discoverer of America in Western popular culture, his historical legacy is more nuanced.

After settling Iceland, the Norse settled the uninhabited southern part of Greenland beginning in the 10th century. Norsemen are believed to have then set sail from Greenland and Iceland to become the first known Europeans to reach the North American mainland, nearly 500 years before Columbus reached the Caribbean.

The 1960s discovery of a Norse settlement dating to c. 1000 AD at L'Anse aux Meadows, Newfoundland, partially corroborates accounts within the Icelandic sagas of Erik the Red's colonization of Greenland and his son Leif Erikson's subsequent exploration of a place he called Vinland.

In the 19th century, amid a revival of interest in Norse culture, Carl Christian Rafn and Benjamin Franklin DeCosta wrote works establishing that the Norse had preceded Columbus in colonizing the Americas.

Following this, in 1874 Rasmus Bjørn Anderson argued that Columbus must have known of the North American continent before he started his voyage of discovery.

Most modern scholars doubt Columbus had knowledge of the Norse settlements in America, with his arrival to the continent being most likely an independent discovery.

Europeans planned explanations for the origins of the Native Americans and their geographical distribution with narratives that often served to reinforce their own preconceptions built on ancient intellectual foundations.

In modern Latin America, the non-Native populations of some countries often demonstrate an unclear attitude toward the perspectives of indigenous peoples regarding the so-called "discovery" by Columbus and the era of colonialism that followed.

In his 1960 monograph, Mexican philosopher and historian Edmundo O'Gorman explicitly rejects the Columbus discovery myth, arguing that the idea that Columbus discovered America was a misleading legend fixed in the public mind through the works of American author Washington Irving during the 19th century.

O'Gorman argues that to assert Columbus "discovered America" is to shape the facts concerning the events of 1492 to make them conform to an interpretation that arose many years later.

For him, the Eurocentric view of the discovery of America sustains systems of domination in ways that favor Europeans.

In a 1992 article for The UNESCO Courier, Félix Fernández-Shaw argues that the word "discovery" prioritizes European explorers as the "heroes" of the contact between the Old and New World. He suggests that the word "encounter" is more appropriate, being a more universal term, which includes Native Americans in the narrative.

CHAPTER 15

America as a Separate Land

Historians have traditionally argued that Columbus remained convinced until his death that his journeys had been along the east coast of Asia as he originally intended, excluding arguments such as Anderson's.

On his third voyage he briefly referred to South America as a "hitherto unknown" continent, while also rationalizing that it was the "Earthly Paradise" located "at the end of the Orient".

Columbus continued to claim in his later writings that he had reached Asia; in a 1502 letter to Pope Alexander VI, he asserts that Cuba is the east coast of Asia.

On the other hand, in a document in the Book of Privileges, 1502, Columbus refers to the New World as the <u>Indias Occidentales</u> 'West Indies', which he says, "were unknown to all the world".

Washington Irving's 1828 biography of Columbus popularized the idea that Columbus had difficulty obtaining support for his plan because many Catholic theologians insisted that the Earth was flat, but this is a popular misconception which can be traced back to 17th-century <u>Protestants campaigning against Catholicism.</u>

In fact, the spherical shape of the Earth had been known to scholars since antiquity, and was common knowledge among sailors, including Columbus.

Coincidentally, the oldest surviving globe of the Earth, the Erdapfel, was made in 1492, just before Columbus's return to Europe from his first voyage. As such it contains no sign of the Americas and yet demonstrates the common belief in a spherical Earth.

Making observations with a quadrant on his third voyage, Columbus inaccurately measured the polar radius of the North Star's diurnal motion to be five degrees, double the value of another erroneous reading he had made from further north. This led him to describe the figure of the Earth as pear-shaped, with the "stalk" portion ascending towards Heaven.

In fact, the Earth ever so slightly is pear-shaped, with its "stalk" pointing north.

Columbus is criticized both for his brutality and for initiating the depopulation of the indigenous peoples of the Caribbean, whether by imported diseases or intentional violence. According to scholars of Native American history, George Tinker and Mark Freedman, Columbus was responsible for creating a cycle of "murder, violence, and slavery" to maximize exploitation of the Caribbean islands' resources, and that

Native deaths on the scale at which they occurred would not have been caused by new diseases alone. Further, they describe the proposition that disease and not genocide caused these deaths as "American holocaust denial".

Other scholars defend Columbus's actions or allege that the worst accusations against him are not based in fact while others claim that "he has been blamed for events far beyond his own reach or knowledge".

As a result of the protests and riots that followed the murder of George Floyd in 2020, many public monuments of Christopher Columbus have been removed.

CHAPTER 16

Brutality

The remains of the pedestal base of the Columbus statue in the Baltimore inner harbor area. The statue was thrown into the harbor on 4 July 2020, as part of the George Floyd protests.

Some historians have criticized Columbus for initiating the widespread colonization of the Americas and for abusing its native population.

Columbus's friend Michele da Cuneo, according to his own account. kept an indigenous woman he captured, whom Columbus "gave to, him", then brutally raped her.

The punishment for an indigenous person, aged 14 and older, failing to pay a hawk's bell, or cascabela, worth of gold dust every six months, based on Bartolomé de las Casas's account, was cutting off the hands of those without tokens, often leaving them to bleed to death.

Columbus had an economic interest in the enslavement of the Hispaniola natives and for that reason was not eager to baptize them, which attracted criticism from some churchmen. Consuelo Varela, a Spanish historian who has seen Bobadilla's report, states that "Columbus's government was characterized by a form of tyranny. Even those who loved him had to admit the atrocities that had taken place."

Kris Lane disputes whether it is appropriate to use the term "genocide" when the atrocities were not Columbus's intent, but resulted from his decrees, family business goals, and negligence.

Other historians have argued that some of the accounts of the brutality of Columbus and his brothers have been exaggerated as part of the Black Legend, a historical tendency towards anti-Spanish sentiment in historical sources dating as far back as the 16th century, which they speculate may continue to taint scholarship into the present day.

According to historian Emily Berquist Soule, the immense Portuguese profits from the maritime trade in African slaves along the West African coast served as an inspiration for Columbus to create a counterpart of this apparatus in the New World using indigenous American slaves.

Historian William J. Connell has argued that while Columbus "brought the entrepreneurial form of slavery to the New World," this "was a phenomenon of the times," further arguing that "we have to be very careful about applying 20th-century understandings of morality to the morality of the 15th century."

In a less popular defense of colonization, Spanish ambassador María Jesús Figa López-Palop has argued, "Normally we melded with the cultures in America, we stayed there, we spread our language and culture and religion."

British historian Basil Davidson has dubbed Columbus the "father of the slave trade", citing the fact that the first license to ship enslaved Africans to the Caribbean was issued by the Catholic Monarchs in 1501 to the first royal governor of Hispaniola, Nicolás de Ovando.

Around the turn of the 21st century, estimates for the pre-Columbian population of Hispaniola ranged between 250,000 and two million, but genetic analysis published in late 2020 suggests that smaller figures are more likely, perhaps as low as 10,000–50,000 for Hispaniola and Puerto Rico combined.

Based on the previous figures of a few hundred thousand, some have estimated that a third or more of the natives in Haiti were dead within the first two years of Columbus's governorship. Contributors to depopulation included disease, warfare, and harsh enslavement.

Indirect evidence suggests that some serious illness may have arrived with the 1,500 colonists who accompanied Columbus' second expedition in 1493.

Charles C. Mann writes that "It was as if the suffering these diseases had caused in Eurasia over the past millennia were concentrated into the span of decades." A third of the natives forced to work in gold and silver mines died every six months.

Within three to six decades, the surviving Arawak population numbered only in the hundreds.

The indigenous population of the Americas overall is thought to have been reduced by about 90% in the century after Columbus's arrival.

Among indigenous peoples, Columbus is often viewed as a key agent of genocide.

Samuel Eliot Morison, a Harvard historian and author of a multivolume biography on Columbus, writes, "The cruel policy initiated by Columbus and pursued by his successors resulted in complete genocide."

Europeans devised explanations for the origins of the Native Americans and their geographical distribution with narratives that often served to reinforce their own preconceptions built on ancient intellectual foundations.

In modern Latin America, the non-Native populations of some countries often demonstrate an ambiguous attitude toward the perspectives of indigenous peoples regarding the so-called "discovery" by Columbus and the era of colonialism that followed.

In his 1960 monograph, Mexican philosopher and historian Edmundo O'Gorman explicitly rejects the Columbus discovery myth, arguing that the idea that Columbus discovered America was a misleading legend fixed in the public mind through the works of American author Washington Irving during the 19th century. O'Gorman argues that to assert Columbus "discovered America" is to shape the facts concerning the events of 1492 to make them conform to an interpretation that arose many years later.

For him, the Eurocentric view of the discovery of America sustains systems of domination in ways that favor Europeans.

In a 1992 article for The UNESCO Courier, Félix Fernández-Shaw argues that the word "discovery" prioritizes European explorers as the "heroes" of the contact between the Old and New World. He suggests that the word "encounter" is more appropriate, being a more universal term, which includes Native Americans in the narrative.

CHAPTER 17

Criticism and Defense

Columbus is criticized both for his brutality and for initiating the depopulation of the indigenous peoples of the Caribbean, whether by imported diseases or intentional violence.

According to scholars of Native American history, George Tinker and Mark Freedman, Columbus was responsible for creating a cycle of "murder, violence, and slavery" to maximize exploitation of the Caribbean islands' resources, and that Native deaths on the scale at which they occurred would not have been caused by new diseases alone.

Further, they describe the proposition that disease and not genocide caused these deaths as "American holocaust denial".

Other scholars defend Columbus's actions or allege that the worst accusations against him are not based in fact while others claim that "he has been blamed for events far beyond his own reach or knowledge".

As a result of the protests and riots that followed the murder of George Floyd in 2020, many public monuments of Christopher Columbus have been removed.

CHAPTER 18

Brutality

The remains of the pedestal base of the Columbus statue in the Baltimore inner harbor area. The statue was thrown into the harbor on 4 July 2020, as part of the George Floyd protests.

Some historians have criticized Columbus for initiating the widespread colonization of the Americas and for abusing its native population.

On St. Croix further explanation needed, Columbus's friend Michele da Cuneo, according to his own account, kept an indigenous woman he captured, whom Columbus "gave to, him", then brutally raped her.

The punishment for an indigenous person, aged 14 and older, failing to pay a hawk's bell, or cascabela, worth of gold dust every six months (based on Bartolomé de las Casas's account) was cutting off the hands of those without tokens, often leaving them to bleed to death.

Columbus had an economic interest in the enslavement of the Hispaniola natives and for that reason was not eager to baptize them, which attracted criticism from some churchmen. Consuelo Varela, a Spanish historian who has seen Bobadilla's report, states that "Columbus's government was characterized by a form of tyranny. Even those who loved him had to admit the crimes that had taken place."

Kris Lane disputes whether it is appropriate to use the term "genocide" when the atrocities were not Columbus's intent, but resulted from his decrees, family business goals, and negligence.

Other historians have argued that some of the accounts of the brutality of Columbus and his brothers have been exaggerated as part of the Black Legend, a historical tendency towards anti-Spanish sentiment in historical sources dating as far back as the 16th century, which they speculate may continue to taint scholarship into the present day.

According to historian Emily Berquist Soule, the immense Portuguese profits from the maritime trade in African slaves along the West African coast served as an inspiration for Columbus to create a counterpart of this apparatus in the New World using indigenous American slaves.

Historian William J. Connell has argued that while Columbus "brought the entrepreneurial form of slavery to the New World," this "was a phenomenon of the times," further arguing that "we have to be very careful about applying 20th-century understandings of morality to the morality of the 15th century."

In a less popular defense of colonization, Spanish ambassador María Jesús Figa López-Palop has argued, "Normally we melded with the cultures in America, we stayed there, we spread our language and culture and religion."

British historian Basil Davidson has dubbed Columbus the "father of the slave trade", citing the fact that the first license to ship enslaved Africans to the Caribbean was issued by the Catholic Monarchs in 1501 to the first royal governor of Hispaniola, Nicolás de Ovando.

CHAPTER 19

The Taínos § Their Depopulation

About the turn of the 21st century, the estimation of the pre-Columbian population of Hispaniola ranged between 250,000 and two million, but genetic analysis published in late 2020 suggested that smaller figures are more likely. It was as low as 10,000–50,000 for both the Hispaniola and Puerto Rico.

Based on the previous figures of a few hundred thousand, some have estimated that a third or more of the natives in Haiti were dead within the first two years of Columbus's governorship.

Contributors to depopulation included disease, warfare, and harsh enslavement. Indirect evidence suggests that some serious illness may have arrived with the 1,500 colonists who accompanied Columbus' second expedition in 1493.

Charles C. Mann writes that "It was as if the suffering these diseases had caused in Eurasia over the past millennia were concentrated into the span of decades."

A third of the natives forced to work in gold and silver mines died every six months. Within three to six decades, the surviving Arawak population numbered only in the hundreds.

The indigenous population of the Americas overall is thought to have been reduced by about 90% in the century after Columbus's arrival.

Among indigenous peoples, Columbus is often viewed as a key agent of extermination.

Samuel Eliot Morison, a Harvard historian and author of a multivolume biography on Columbus, writes, "The cruel policy initiated by Columbus and pursued by his successors resulted in complete extermination."

According to Noble David Cook, "There were too few Spaniards to have killed the millions who were reported to have died in the first century after Old and New World contact." He instead estimates that the death toll was caused by smallpox, which may have caused a pandemic only after the arrival of Hernán Cortés in 1519.

Some estimated, that smallpox had an 80–90% fatality rate in Native American populations. The natives had no acquired immunity to these new diseases and suffered high fatalities. There is also evidence that they had poor diets and were overworked.

Historian Andrés Reséndez of University of California, Davis, says the available evidence suggests "slavery has emerged as major killer" of the indigenous populations of the Caribbean between 1492 and 1550 more so than diseases such as smallpox, influenza, and malaria.

He said that indigenous populations did not experience a rebound like European populations did following the Black Death because unlike their final, a large portion of the former were subjected to deadly forced labor in the mines.

The diseases that devastated the Native Americans came in multiple waves at different times, sometimes as much as centuries apart, which would mean that survivors of one disease may have been killed by others, preventing the population from recovering.

Historian David Stannard describes the depopulation of the indigenous Americans as "neither inadvertent nor inevitable," saying it was the result of both disease and intentional genocide.

Biographers and historians have a wide range of opinions about Columbus's expertise. His experience navigating and captaining ships was amazing.

Some scholars stating differently. European works ranging from the 1890s to 1980s that support Columbus's experience and skill as among the best in Genoa, while listing some American works over a similar timeframe that portray the explorer as an untrained entrepreneur, having only minor crew or passenger experience prior to his noted journeys.

According to Morison, Columbus's success in utilizing the trade winds might owe significantly to luck.

Contemporary descriptions of Columbus, including those by his son Fernando and Bartolomé de las Casas, describe him as taller than average, with light skin, which was often sunburnt, blue, or hazel eyes, high cheekbones and freckled face, an curved nose, and blond to reddish hair and beard, until about the age of 30, when it began to whiten.

One Spanish commentator described his eyes using the word garzos, now usually translated as "light blue", but it seems to have indicated light grey-green or hazel eyes to Columbus's contemporaries. The word rubios can mean "blond", "fair", or "ruddy".

Although an abundance of artwork depicts Christopher Columbus, no authentic contemporary portrait is known.

The most well-known image of Columbus is a portrait by Sebastiano del Piombo, which has been reproduced in many textbooks. It agrees with descriptions of Columbus in that it shows a large man with auburn hair, but the painting dates from 1519 and cannot, therefore, have been painted from life.

Furthermore, the inscription identifying the subject as Columbus was probably added later, and the face shown differs from that of other images.

Sometime between 1531 and 1536, Alejo Fernández painted an altarpiece, The Virgin of the Navigators, that includes a depiction of

Columbus. The painting was commissioned for a chapel in Seville's <u>Casa de Contratación,</u> House of Trade, in the Alcázar of Seville and remains there.

At the World's Columbian Exposition in 1893, 71 alleged portraits of Columbus were displayed; most of them did not match contemporary descriptions.

CHAPTER 20

Christopher Columbus Dies

On May 20, 1506, the Italian explorer Christopher Columbus dies in Valladolid, Spain. Columbus was the first European to explore the Americas since the Vikings set up colonies in Greenland and Newfoundland in the 10th century.

He explored the West Indies, South America, and Central America, but died a disappointed man, feeling he had been mistreated by his patron, King Ferdinand of Spain.

Columbus was born in Genoa, Italy, in 1451. Little is known of his early life, but he worked as a seaman and then a sailing entrepreneur. He became obsessed with the possibility of pioneering a western sea route to Cathay, China, India, and the mythical gold and spice islands of Asia.

At the time, Europeans knew no direct sea route to southern Asia, and the route via Egypt and the Red Sea was closed to Europeans by the Ottoman Empire, as were many land routes.

Contrary to popular legend, educated Europeans of Columbus' day did believe that the world was round, as argued by St. Isidore in the seventh century. However, Columbus, and most others, underestimated the world's size, calculating that East Asia must lie approximately where North America sits on the globe, they did not yet know that the Pacific Ocean existed.

With only the Atlantic Ocean, he thought, lying between Europe and the riches of the East Indies, Columbus met with King John II of

Portugal and tried to persuade him to back his "Enterprise of the Indies," as he called his plan.

He was rejected and went to Spain, where he was also denied at least twice by King Ferdinand and Queen Isabella. However, after the Spanish conquest of the Moorish kingdom of Granada in January 1492, the Spanish monarchs, flush with victory, agreed to support his voyage.

On August 3, 1492, Columbus set sail from Palos, Spain, with three small ships, the Santa Maria, the Pinta, and the Nina.

On October 12, the expedition spotted land, probably Watling Island in the Bahamas, and went ashore the same day, claiming it for Spain. Later that month, Columbus sighted Cuba, which he thought was mainland China, and in December the expedition landed on Hispaniola, which Columbus thought might be Japan. He established a small colony there with 39 of his men.

The explorer returned to Spain with gold, spices, and "Indian" captives in March 1493, and was received with the highest honors by the Spanish court. He was given the title "admiral of the ocean sea," and a second expedition was promptly organized.

Fitted out with a large fleet of 17 ships, with 1,500 colonists aboard, Columbus set out from Cadiz in September 1493 on his second voyage to the New World. Landfall was made in the Lesser Antilles in November.

When Columbus returned to Hispaniola, he found the men he left there slaughtered by the natives, and he founded a second colony.

Sailing on, he explored Puerto Rico, Jamaica, and numerous smaller islands in the Caribbean. Columbus returned to Spain in June 1496 and was greeted less warmly, as the yield from the second voyage had fallen well short of its costs.

Isabella and Ferdinand, still greedy for the riches of the East, agreed to a smaller third voyage and instructed Columbus to find a strait to India.

In May 1498, Columbus left Spain with six ships, three filled with colonists and three with provisions for the colony on Hispaniola. This time, he made landfall on Trinidad. He entered the Gulf of Paria in Venezuela and planted the Spanish flag on South America.

By the possibility of the Orinoco River in Venezuela, he realized he had stumbled upon another continent, which Columbus, a deeply religious man, decided after careful thought was the outer regions of the Garden of Eden.

As he returned to Hispaniola, he found that conditions on the island had deteriorated under the rule of his brothers, Diego, and Bartholomew. Columbus' efforts to restore order were marked by brutality, and his rule came to be deeply resented by both the colonists and the native Taino chiefs.

In 1500, Spanish chief justice Francisco de Bobadilla arrived at Hispaniola, sent by Isabella and Ferdinand to investigate complaints, and Columbus and his brother were sent back to Spain in chains.

He was immediately released upon his return, and Ferdinand and Isabella agreed to finance a fourth voyage in which he was to search for the earthly paradise and the realms of gold said to lie nearby. He was also to continue looking for a passage to India.

In May 1502, Columbus left Cadiz on his fourth and final voyage to the New World. After returning to Hispaniola against his patron's wishes, he explored the coast of Central America looking for a strait and for gold. Attempting to return to Hispaniola, his ships, in poor condition, had to be beached on Jamaica.

Columbus and his men were deserted, but two of his captains succeed in canoeing the 450 miles to Hispaniola. Columbus was a castaway on Jamaica for a year before a rescue ship arrived.

In November 1504, Columbus returned to Spain. Queen Isabella, his chief patron, died less than three weeks later.

Although Columbus enjoyed a substantial revenue from Hispaniola gold during the last years of his life, he repeatedly attempted, unsuccessfully, to gain an audience with King Ferdinand, whom he felt owed him further redress. Columbus died on May 20, 1506.

CHAPTER 21

Accomplishments of Christopher Columbus

The colonist who played a key role in shaping the history of the world as it was his voyages that initiated widespread contact between the Old World, and the New World.

Columbus was born in the Republic of Genoa and lived in Portugal before eventually going on to settle in Spain. Columbus wanted to find a sea route to Asia by sailing across the Atlantic. He was not successful in his endeavor but ended up leading the first European expeditions to the Caribbean, Central America, and South America.

His voyages were beneficial for Europe and made possible the colonization of the Americas. Columbus was responsible for the Columbian Exchange, an event that changed the history of mankind.

There are numerous negative aspects of the effects of his voyages as well as in his personal life. He regularly used torture and mutilation to govern Hispaniola.

Columbus promoted slavery; and his voyages ultimately led to the extinction of the civilizations of the Americas. Even with so many negativities, he did accomplish a lot for both America and Spain.

Christopher Columbus independently discovered the Americas. It was nearly impossible in the 15th century to head into Asia from Europe via land. The route was long and laden with hostile armies.

While the Portuguese explorers were solving this quandary by sailing across the West African coast and around the Cape of Good Hope, Columbus put forth the notion of sailing across the Atlantic.

The plans Columbus had been however based on faulty European mathematics. He calculated the circumference of the earth as much smaller than it was and thought that the proposed journey would be easy to complete.

Though his calculations were faulty, and he never discovered an alternate route to Asia, Columbus ended up independently discovering the Americas.

Though he was not the first to discover the Americas, it was his voyage that redefined history and was instrumental in initiating centuries of conquest and colonization, asserting Europe's dominance over the world.

It was Columbus who discovered a viable sailing route to the Americas. He started his career by serving as an apprentice to some of the most influential families in Genoa. He eventually went on to be recognized as a seagoing entrepreneur.

Columbus sailed to Iceland and Ireland with the merchant marine in 1477 and was trading sugar in Madeira by 1478 as an agent for the Genoese firm of Centurioni.

Then, after years of lobbying, Columbus's plan to discover an alternate route to Asia was sponsored by the Catholic Monarchs of Spain. They hoped that he would discover a route to China and India, that were famous for their spices and gold, among other things.

Columbus left Spain in August 1492 with three ships: the Nina, the Pinta and the Santa Maria. He made landfall in the Americas on October 12, 1492, in the Bahama Islands.

Though not known to him then, Columbus had reached the eastern coast of the Americas, a continent which was not then known to the Old World. Though he was not the first man to discover the Americas,

Columbus did find a viable sailing route to the Americas, which was no mean achievement.

Without even knowing was he was going to face, Columbus led the frs European expeditions to the Caribbean, Central America, and South America.

Christopher Columbus undertook three more expeditionary voyages from Spain to the New World. His second voyage began on September 24, 1493, with a fleet of 17 ships carrying 1,200 men.

The expedition contained supplies to establish permanent colonies in the New World. In November 1493 his crew saw land and discovered the Dominica, Guadeloupe, and Jamaica islands. In March 1496, he set sail back to Spain.

On May 30, 1498, Columbus left with six ships for his third trip to the New World. In July, the same year, he landed on the island of Trinidad. He then explored the Gulf of Paria and finally touched South America.

Due to bad health, he returned to Hispaniola on August 19, 1498. The fourth voyage of Columbus began in May 1502.

During this voyage he reached Central America. He sailed back to Spain in 1504. Columbus thus led the first European expeditions to the Caribbean, Central America, and South America.

Columbus settlement in Hispaniola provided Spain strategic advantage for expansion in the new world.

The four voyages Columbus provided a overabundance of information to the Europeans about sailing from Europe to the Americas; as well as about the various kinds of people who resided in the New World.

A side from the information gathered from his voyages, another important consequence of his expeditions was the island of Hispaniola.

Founded by Columbus on his voyages in 1492 and 1493, Hispaniola was the site of the first permanent European settlement in the Americas.

This ultimately aided Spain in its conquest of the west as the island's position in the northern side of the Caribbean Sea proved to be a strategic standpoint for the expansion of Spain to Cuba, Mexico, Panama, and South America.

Columbus made colonization possible for Spain. His efforts as an explorer, set forth a chain of events that allowed Spain to establish a permanent foothold on the American continents.

Spain started this by destroying the Aztecs, the Incas, and the Mayan cultures, which paved way for 500 years of Western domination.

In essence, Columbus's voyages resulted in an everlasting contact between the Western and Eastern hemispheres of the world.

While this resulted in the destruction of the native people of the Americas, it proved to be the basis on which our modern world is built.

Led by Spain, the Europeans gained exceedingly due to the efforts of Columbus helping them prosper at the expense of their colonies and paving the way for their domination of the modern world.

Columbian Exchange is a term coined by Alfred W. Crosby in his revolutionary book The Columbian Exchange which was published in 1972.

The term refers to the widespread exchange of animals, plants, human populations, diseases, technology, and ideas that occurred between Afro-Eurasia and the Americas after Christopher Columbus landed in the New World.

For instance, potatoes, corn, and tomatoes were introduced to the Old World. Similarly, cattle, hogs and sheep were introduced to the people of America. The Columbian Exchange is one of the most important events in the history of mankind which had a great impact on the world in numerous ways.

Thus, in a way, Columbus altered the history of mankind through his voyages.

Prior to the Columbian Exchange, the Old World had never seen a catfish or a tomato while the Native Americans had never seen a cow or an apple.

Due to the Columbian Exchange, a lot of crops and animals were introduced to both Old and New World. Crops introduced to Old World include potato, tomato, maize, cacao, and tobacco. Crops introduced to New World include rice, wheat, apples, bananas, and coffee.

Turkey and Llama are probably the only prominent New World domesticated animals which were introduced to the Old World. However, many animals were imported to the New World including horses, cows, chickens, donkeys, and pigs. These animals, especially pigs because they breed very quickly, expanded the food supply in the Americas.

The plants from the Americas had a huge impact on the Old World. Lives of millions of people in Africa, Europe and Asia were changed radically due to the introduction of New World crops. New World plants like potatoes and maize could grow in soils which were useless for Old World crops.

Today China and India are the largest producers and consumers of potatoes in the world. Cassava provides more calories than any plant on earth and is the basic diet of more than half a million people in the developing world.

As the crops from the Americas were far more caloric than Old World food it led to probably the greatest population increase the world had ever seen. Between 1650 and 1850 the population of the world doubled.

Christopher Columbus was widely regarded as an expert navigator and maritime explorer of his time. He held many important titles and positions during his lifetime.

In 1492, Columbus received the title of "Almirante mayor del Mar Oceano" which translates to "Admiral of the Ocean". Columbus had a legal agreement with the Spanish Crown that entitled him to a percentage of their profits from his discoveries.

He was also granted the viceroyalty and governorship of any lands that he might discover. Following his first voyage, Columbus was appointed Viceroy and Governor of the Indies. In effect, this meant that he was given power to administer the colonies in the island of Hispaniola.

He held this title from 1492 to 1499, after which he was dismissed due to accusations of tyranny and incompetence.

Christopher Columbus is regarded as one of the most prominent figures in Spanish history. His contribution has been commemorated via a monument that stands as a tall pillar pointing towards the sea in Barcelona.

In addition to this, Columbus Day is celebrated in America on the second Monday of October. While he was unable to fulfil his dream of finding a new passage to Asia, Christopher Columbus' voyages gave headway to events that shaped the world for hundreds of years. I

In this regard, he is considered one of the most influential explorers in history.

Although it can't be established certainly how many Native Americans died due to the arrival of Europeans, but it is estimated that 80-95 percent died in the 150 years following the arrival of Columbus.

The most affected regions lost 100 percent of their indigenous population. Though European brutality was a factor, the primary reason behind this were the diseases introduced to the New World through Columbian Exchange like smallpox, measles, malaria, typhus, chicken pox and yellow fever.

Also due to the Columbian Exchange, the diversity of life on earth has reduced drastically and planting crops where they don't belong has hurt the environment.

Man and "the plants and animals that he brought with him have caused the extinction of more species of life forms in the last four hundred years than the usual processes of evolution might kill off in a million".

CHAPTER 22

Coming to America

Who discovered America? Is the famous question some Americans may still ask.

For most of us, the answer to that question is straightforward, Christopher Columbus. That's what we were taught in school and that is why we celebrate Columbus Day. Yet it is far from clear-cut.

There are many theories about who got here first. Author Russell Freedom explores the various contenders for the title of "first" in his new book, Who Was First? Discovering the Americas. He shares his insights with NPR.

When you started searching for answers, were you like the rest of us? Did you believe that Christopher Columbus discovered America and that was it, end of story?

I was aware of the Vikings. But really, what provoked my interest was a book called 1421: The Year China Discovered America. That book has been largely discredited, but what is clear is that there have been successive waves of immigration to the Western Hemisphere from outside.

Where they came from and when they arrived and how they got here, that's all still speculative.

Tell me about the Irish Monks who supposedly preceded even the Vikings.

That falls into the realm of legend. But it's possible that they came across the North Sea, to what is now Newfoundland, before the Vikings. No one knows for sure.

What happened with the Vikings?

That is well established. I searched for some answers. There is no question about it. It has been determined that the Vikings were there for about 10 years specifically, Leif Erikson and his extended family.

Is there any physical evidence that remains today?

Yes, the remains of their houses, of their settlement. There was an archeological dig that lasted six or seven years, and then they reconstructed the settlement about 100 yards away.

What did Leif Erikson make of this New World?

It was full of wonderful resources: timber and grapes. Coming from Greenland, as he did, which had no timber or grapes to make wine, these were two priceless discoveries. That's why the Vikings called it "Vinland" or Wine Land.

If it was so wonderful, why didn't the Vikings stay longer?

The Indians didn't want them to stay. The first encounter was when the Vikings came across 10 Indians taking naps under their overturned canoes and the Vikings killed them. That did not set up a very good mutual relationship.

There were some attempts at trading, but the Vikings felt quite menaced and outnumbered, and the Indians did not appreciate their presence. The Vikings did return to North America, but only for trading. They never settled again.

What about the "China first" theory? Is there any evidence to support the notion that Chinese mariners set foot in America before Columbus?

There is credible evidence that a Chinese fleet went as far as the coast of Africa, in present-day Kenya. It was the largest maritime fleet in the world, under the command of Zheng He, a favorite of the emperor.

Whether the fleet went around the horn of Africa and then across the Atlantic is speculative.

The theory has been widely shot down by experts in the field. There is no real evidence. The author uses a grab bag of evidence, some of it is suggestive and some of it is ridiculous.

If Columbus wasn't first, why does he get all the credit?

He opened America to Europe, which was the expansionist power at the time. He was the one who made it possible for them to conquer the Western Hemisphere and to bring with them the diseases that apparently wiped-out 90 percent of the population.

He wasn't the first, and neither were the Vikings, that is a very Eurocentric view. There were millions of people here already, and so their ancestors must have been the first.

What did you find most surprising in researching this book?

For one thing, the longevity of settlement of the Western Hemisphere 20,000 years, at least. I don't think it's silly, this quest for answers of who got here first. You always want to know what happened before you. It' a human instinct to know where you came from and what proceeded you.

How did they get here? Who were they? The fact that we don't know for sure makes it quite fascinating.

Before Columbus......

For a long time, most people believed that Christopher Columbus was the first explorer to "discover" America and the first to make a successful round-trip voyage across the Atlantic.

In recent years, as new evidence came to light, our understanding of history has changed. We know now that Columbus was among the last explorers to reach the Americas, not the first.

Five hundred years before Columbus, a daring band of Vikings led by Leif Eriksson set foot in North America and established a settlement.

Long before that, some scholars say, the Americas seem to have been visited by seafaring travelers from China, and possibly by visitors from Africa and even Ice Age Europe.

A popular legend suggests an additional event:

According to an ancient manuscript, a band of Irish monks led by Saint Brendan sailed an ox-hide boat westward in the sixth century in search of new lands.

After seven years, they returned home and reported that they had discovered a land covered with luxuriant vegetation, believed by some people today to have been Newfoundland.

All along, of course, the two continents we now call North and South America had already been "discovered." Before European explorers arrived, the Americas were home to tens of millions of native peoples.

While those Native American groups differed greatly from one another, they all performed rituals and ceremonies, songs, and dances, that brought back to mind and heart memories of the ancestors who had come before them and given them their place on Earth.

Who were the ancestors of those Native Americans? Where did they come from, when did they arrive in the Americas, and how did they make their epic journeys?

As we dig deeper and deeper into the past, we find that the Americas have always been lands of immigrants, lands that have been "discovered" time and again by different peoples coming from different parts of the world over the course of countless generations going far back to the prehistoric past, when a band of Stone Age hunters first set foot in what truly was an unexplored New World.

Christopher Columbus was having trouble with his crew. His fleet of three small sailing ships had left the Canary Islands nearly three weeks earlier, heading west across the uncharted Ocean Sea, as the Atlantic was known. He had expected to reach China or Japan by now, but there was still no sign of land.

None of the sailors had ever been so long away from the sight of land, and as the days passed, they grew increasingly restless and fearful. The Ocean Sea was known also as the Sea of Darkness.

Ugly monsters were said to prowl beneath the waves poisonous sea serpents and giant crabs that could rise from the deep and crush a ship along with its crew.

If the Earth was flat, as many of the men believed, then they might fall off the edge of the world and plunge into that fiery abyss where the sun sets in the west.

What's more, Columbus was a foreigner and a red-headed Italian commanding a crew of tough seafaring Spaniards. That meant he couldn't be trusted.

Finally, the men demanded that Columbus turn back and head for home. When he refused, some of the sailors whispered together of mutiny. They wanted to kill the admiral by throwing him overboard.

But, for the moment, the crisis has passed. Columbus managed to calm his men and persuade them to be patient a while longer.

"I am having serious trouble with the crew . . . complaining that they will never be able to return home," he wrote in his journal. "They have said that it is insanity and suicidal on their part to risk their lives following the madness of a foreigner. . . .. I am told by a few trusted men, and these are few! that if I persist in going onward, the best course of action will be to throw me into the sea some night."

All along, Columbus had been keeping two sets of logs. One, which he kept secretly and showed to no one, was accurate, recording the distance really sailed each day.

The other log, which he showed to his crew, hoping to reassure them that they were nowhere near the edge of the world, deliberately underestimated the miles they had covered since leaving Spain.

They sailed on for another two weeks and still saw nothing. There were more rumblings of protest and complaint from the crew. The men seemed willing to endure no more.

On October 10, Columbus announced that he would give a fine silk coat to the man who first sighted land. The sailors greeted that offer with glum silence. What good was a silk coat in the middle of the Sea of Darkness?

Later that day, Columbus spotted a flock of birds flying toward the southwest a sign that land was close. He ordered his ships to follow the birds.

The next night, the moon rose in the east shortly before midnight. About two hours later, at two A.M. on October 12, a sailor on one of Columbus's ships, the Pinta, saw a white stretch of beach, shouted, "Land! Land!" and fired a cannon.

At dawn, the three ships dropped anchor in the calm, blue waters just offshore. They had arrived at an island in what we now call the Bahamas.

Excited crew members crowded the decks. People were standing on the beach, waiting to greet them. The natives had no weapons other than wooden fishing spears, and they were practically naked. Who were these people? And what place was this?

Columbus supposed that his fleet had landed on one of the many islands that Marco Polo had reported lay just off the coast of Asia. They must have reached the Indies, he thought islands apparently near India and known today as the East Indies.

He decided that those people on the beach must be "Indians," the name by which they have been known ever since. China and Japan, he believed, lay a bit farther to the north.

Though Christopher Columbus was an Italian born in Genoa, he had lived for years in Portugal, where he worked as a bookseller, a mapmaker, and a sailor. He had sailed on Portuguese voyages as far as Iceland in the North Atlantic, and down the coast of Africa in the South Atlantic.

During his days at sea, he read books on history, geography, and travel...

Like most educated people at the time, Columbus believed that the Earth was round, not flat, as some ignorant folks still insisted. The Ocean Sea was seen as a great expanse of water surrounding the land mass of Eurasia and Africa, which stretched from Europe in the west to China and Japan in the far distant east.

If a ship left the coast of Europe, sailed west toward the setting sun, and circled the globe, it would reach the shores of Asia or so Columbus thought.

In the past, European explorers and traders had taken the overland route to the Far East, with its precious silks and spices. They traveled for months by horse and camel along the Silk Road, an ancient caravan trail that crossed deserts and climbed dizzying mountain peaks.

Marco Polo had followed the Silk Road on his famous journey to China two centuries earlier. But recently, this land route to Asia, controlled in part by the Turks, had been closed to Europeans. And in any case, Columbus was convinced that he could find an easier and faster route to Asia by sailing west.

There were plenty of stories circulating in those years about the possibility of sailing directly from Europe to Asia, an idea first considered by the ancient Greeks.

Columbus owned a book called Imago Mundi, or Image of the World, by a French scholar, Pierre d'Ailly, who argued that the Ocean Sea wasn't as wide as it seemed and that a ship driven by favorable winds could cross it in a few days.

Next to that passage in the margin of the book, Columbus had written: "There is no reason to think that the ocean covers half the earth."

In 1484, he proposed his bold scheme of sailing west to China to King John II of Portugal, a monarch who had paid much attention to the discovery of new lands.

Portugal was Europe's leading maritime power. Portuguese explorers in search of slaves, ivory, and gold had already discovered rich kingdoms and colossal rivers in western Africa and would soon reach the Cape of Good Hope at Africa's southern tip.

From there, they would be able to sail across the Indian Ocean to the famed Spice Islands of southeast Asia.

King John listened to what Columbus had to say, then submitted the Italian sailor's plan to a committee of mapmakers, astronomers, and geographers. The distinguished experts declared that Asia must be much farther away than Columbus thought.

They said that no expedition could be fitted out with enough food and water to sail across such an enormous expanse of sea.

Rejected by the Portuguese king, Columbus decided to approach King Ferdinand and Queen Isabella of Spain, a country he had never visited. Well-connected friends gave him letters of introduction to the inner circle of the Spanish royal court.

Ferdinand and Isabella seemed curious about the route to Asia that Columbus proposed. Like King John, they too appointed a committee of inquiry to consider the matter, but those experts came to the same negative conclusion: Columbus's claim about the distance to China and the ease of sailing there could not possibly be true.

Columbus persisted. He talked at length to members of the Spanish court and convinced some of them, but Ferdinand and Isabella twice rejected his appeal for ships. Finally, angry, and impatient after six discouraging years in Spain, he threatened to seek support from the king of France. Columbus set out for France, riding a mule down a dusty Spanish road.

With that, royal advisors persuaded Ferdinand and Isabella to change their minds. If another king sponsored Columbus, and his expedition turned out to be a success, then the Spanish monarchs would be embarrassed. They would be criticized in Spain.

Let Columbus risk his life, the advisors said. Let him seek out "the splendors and secrets of the universe." If he succeeded, Spain would win much glory and would overcome the Portuguese lead in the race to exploit the riches of Asia.

So, Ferdinand and Isabella decided to take a chance. They dispatched a messenger to capture Columbus on the road and bring him back to court. They were ready to grant him a hereditary title, Admiral of the Ocean Sea, and the right to a tenth of any riches, pearls, gold, silver, silks, spices that he brought back from his voyage.

They agreed to supply two ships for his expedition. Columbus himself raised the money to hire a third ship.

A half hour before sunrise on August 3, 1492, the Nina, the Pinta, and the Santa María sailed from the port of Palos, Spain, carrying some ninety crew members in all.

They were small, lightweight ships called caravels, swift and maneuverable, each with three masts, their white sails with big red crosses billowing before the wind.

They had on board food that would last, salted cod, bacon, and biscuits, along with flour, wine, olive oil, and plenty of water, enough for a year.

In his small cabin, Columbus kept several hourglasses to mark the passage of time, a compass, and an astrolabe, an instrument for calculating latitude by observing the movement of the sun.

The little fleet stopped for repairs at La Gomera in the Canary Islands, a Spanish possession off the coast of Morocco.

On September 6, 1492, after praying at the parish church of San Sebastian, which still looks out over the ocean today, Columbus and his three ships set sail again, heading due west, moving now through the unknown waters of the Ocean Sea.

Five weeks later, on October 12, 1492, his worried crew finally sighted land....

Columbus called the place where they landed San Salvador, the first of many Caribbean islands that he would name. The natives who greeted him called their island Guanabani.

They themselves were a people known as the Taínos, the largest group of natives inhabiting the islands of what we today call the West Indies.

Columbus tells us a few things about these now-extinct people. He was impressed by their good looks and apparent robust health. "They are very well-built people, with handsome bodies and very fine faces," he wrote in his log. "Their eyes are large and very pretty....

These are tall people and their legs, with no exceptions, are quite straight, and none of them has a paunch." Many of the Taínos had painted their faces or their whole bodies black or white or red.

As Columbus and his men noticed right away, some of them wore gold earrings and nose rings. They offered gifts to the European visitors, parrots, wooden javelins, and balls of cotton thread.

From San Salvador, Columbus sailed on to several more islands, still believing that he was close to Japan "because all my globes and world maps seem to indicate that the island of Japan is in this vicinity." He stopped at Cuba and at Hispaniola, the island that today contains Haiti and the Dominican Republic.

He wrote enthusiastically in his journal of the rich tropical beauty of the islands, the sweet singing of birds "that might make a man wish never to leave here," and the hospitality of the people: "They gave my men bread and fish and whatever they had." And later, "They brought us all they had in this world, knowing what I wanted, and they did it so generously and willingly that it was wonderful."

The Taínos lived in large, airy wooden houses with palm roofs. They slept in cotton hammocks, sat on wooden chairs carved in elaborate animal shapes, and kept small barkless dogs and tame birds as pets.

They were skilled farmers, fishermen, and boat builders who traveled from island to island in long, brightly painted canoes carved from tree trunks, each of which carried as many as 150 people.

They told Columbus that they called themselves Taínos, a word meaning "good," to distinguish themselves from the "bad" Caribs, their fierce, warlike neighbors who raided Taino villages, carried off their girls as brides, and, the Taínos insisted, ate human flesh.

To fend off Carib attacks, the Taínos painted themselves red and fought back with clubs, bows and arrows, and spears propelled by throwing sticks.

The Taínos themselves were not warlike, Columbus reported to his monarchs: "They are an affectionate people, free from greed and agreeable to everything. I certify to Your Highnesses that in all the world I do not believe there is a better people or a better country. They love their neighbors as themselves, and they have the softest and gentlest voices in the world and are always smiling."

A village chief gave Columbus a mask with golden eyes and large ears of gold. The Spaniards were already aware that many of the Taínos wore gold jewelry. They kept asking where the gold came from.

After much searching, they found a river on the island of Hispaniola where "the sand was full of gold, and in such quantity, that it is wonderful. . .. I named this El Rio del Oro", The River of Gold.

Columbus built a small fort nearby and left thirty-nine men behind to collect gold samples and await the next Spanish expedition.

Still believing that he had discovered unknown islands near the shores of Asia, he sailed back to Spain with some gold from Hispaniola and with ten Indians he had kidnapped so he could train them as interpreters and exhibit them at the royal court. One of the Indigenous people died at sea.

He returned to a triumphant welcome. It was said that when Ferdinand and Isabella received him at their court in Barcelona, "there were tears in the royal eyes." They greeted Columbus as a hero, inviting him to ride with them in royal processions.

A second voyage was planned. This time, the monarchs gave Columbus seventeen ships, about fifteen hundred men, and a few women to colonize the islands.

He was instructed to continue his explorations, establish gold mines, install settlers, develop trade with the Indigenous people, and convert them to Christianity.

Columbus returned to Hispaniola in the fall of 1493. He hoped to find massive amounts of gold on the island. To his surprise, the mines produced less gold than expected. The European crops planted by the settlers died in the tropical climate.

Some settlers began to steal from the Indians. They were stealing their possessions, abducting their wives, and seizing captives to be shipped to Spain and sold as slaves.

Thousands of Taínos fled to the mountains to escape capture. Others, vowing to avenge themselves, attacked any Spaniards they found in small groups and set fire to their huts.

While Columbus was a courageous and enterprising mariner, he proved to be a poor governor, unable to control the greed of his followers.

In 1496, he was called back to Spain to answer complaints about his management of the colony.

When he appeared at court before Ferdinand and Isabella, he found the king and queen were still willing to support his explorations.

Columbus gave them a "good sample of gold . . . and many masks, with eyes and ears of gold, and many parrots." He also presented to the monarchs "Diego," the brother of a Taino chief, who was wearing a heavy gold collar.

These hints that more gold might be forthcoming encouraged Ferdinand and Isabella to send Columbus back to the Indies, this time with eight ships.

When he returned to Hispaniola on his third voyage in 1498, he found the island in chaos, torn by conflicts and disagreements among the settlers.

Many colonists, unable to make a living from the gold mines or by farming, were demanding to return to Spain. Others, enemies of Columbus who wanted to gain control of the colony, rebelled against his rule.

When word of the conflict reached Spain, the king and queen sent an emissary, Francisco de Bobadilla, to investigate the uprising and take charge of the government.

Columbus, it seems, made the mistake of arguing with the royal emissary and challenging his credentials. He was promptly arrested and with his two brothers was shipped back to Spain to face charges of wrongdoing. "Bobadilla sent me here in chains," he wrote to Ferdinand and Isabella when he landed in Spain. "I swear that I do not know, nor can I think why."

Though Columbus was quickly pardoned by the Spanish monarchs, who felt he had been treated too harshly, he was stripped of his right to govern the islands he had discovered, and he lost his title as Admiral of the Ocean Sea.

Even so, he was allowed to make one more voyage, sailing across the Caribbean and exploring the coast of Central America. This final expedition was cursed by bad luck.

Two of Columbus's ships became so infested with termites, they sank. When he headed back to Spain, he had to shore his remaining ships at St. Ann's Bay in Jamaica, where he was stranded for a year before being rescued in the fall of 1504. He returned to Spain an ill and disappointed man.

Spanish colonists, meanwhile, had been settling in Hispaniola, Cuba, Puerto Rico, Jamaica, and other islands in the West Indies.

The local Indigenous people were put to work as forced laborers in the goldfields or on Spanish ranches. Indigenous people who resisted were killed, sometimes with terrible brutality, or were shipped to Spain to be sold as slaves.

Spanish missionaries condemned this mistreatment, but with little effect. "I have seen the greatest cruelty and inhumanity practiced on these gentle and peace-loving, native peoples," Father Bartolomé de Las Casas would say a half century later, "without any reason except for greedy, thirst, and hunger for gold."

As the number of Spanish colonists increased, the native population of the West Indies quickly declined. Tens of thousands of native people were worked to death or died of smallpox, measles, and other European diseases to which they had no immunity.

As the Taínos died off, the colonists brought in black slaves from Africa to labor on ranches and in the spreading sugar-cane fields.

Within fifty years, the Taínos had stopped to exist as a distinct race of people. A few Taino words survive today in Spanish and even in English, including hammock, canoe, hurricane, savannah, barbecue, and cannibal.

Columbus died in a Spanish monastery on May 20, 1506, at the age of fifty-seven, still believing that he had found a new route to Asia, and that China and Japan lay just beyond the islands he had explored.

By then, other explorers were following the sea route founded by the Admiral of the Ocean Sea, and Europeans were already speaking of Columbus's discoveries as a "New World."

The first map of the world to show these newly discovered lands across the Ocean Sea appeared in 1507, a year after Christopher Columbus's death.

The mapmaker, Martin Waldseemüller, named the New World "America," after the Italian Amerigo Vespucci, who had explored the coastline of South America and was the first to realize that it was a separate continent, not part of Asia.

Columbus was not the first explorer to "discover" America. His voyages were significant because they were the first to become widely known in Europe. They opened a pathway from the Old World to the New, covering the way for the European conquest and colonization of the Americas, changing life forever on both sides of the Atlantic.

CHAPTER 23

Diego Columbus

Diego Columbus, Portuguese: Diogo Colombo; Spanish: Diego Colón; Italian: Diego Colombo. He was born between 1479-1480 and died on February 23, 1526.

Diego Columbus was a navigator and explorer under the Kings of Castile and Aragón. He served as the 2nd Admiral of the Indies, 2nd Viceroy of the Indies and 4th Governor of the Indies as a vassal to the Kings of Castile and Aragón. He was the eldest son of Christopher Columbus and his wife Filipa Moniz Perestrelo.

He was born in Portugal, either in Porto Santo in 1479-1480, or in Lisbon in 1474. He spent most of his adult life trying to regain the titles and privileges granted to his father for his explorations.

After all his effort, it was denied in 1500. He was greatly aided in this goal by his marriage to María de Toledo y Rojas, niece of the 2nd Duke of Alba, who was the cousin of King Ferdinand.

Diego was made part of the Spanish court in 1492, the year his father boarded on his first voyage. Diego had a younger half-brother, Fernando, by Beatriz Enríquez de Arana.

Diego Columbus's teacher was Beatrice De Arana, Christopher Columbus's second wife, Beatrice De Arana. She taught him until he was transferred to the Franciscan monastery of La Rabida, at the urging of Father Juan Perez and friar Horacio Crassocius, prominent Franciscans, and occasional priests to his father.

Ferdinand and Diego served Prince Don Juan, then they served Queen Isabella in 1497.

In August 1508, he was named Governor of the Indies, the post his father had held, arriving to Santo Domingo in July 1509. He established his home, the Alcázar de Colón, which still stands in Santo Domingo, in what is now the Dominican Republic.

In 1511 as Viceroy of the Indies, Diego Columbus commissioned Diego Velázquez de Cuéllar to go on an expedition from Santo Domingo to the newly acquired Spanish island of Cuba.

According to Floyd, Diego "...was accompanied by a splendid entourage: his wife, Doña Maria, the first gran dama of the New World, the Duke of Alba's niece, with her own suite of doncellas; and his immediate relatives

Fernando his half-brother, his two uncles, Diego and Bartolomé, and his cousins, Andrea, and Giovanni.

Also on the expedition were his criados and his father's old retainers: Marcos de Aguilar, his forthright alcalde mayor, Diego Mendez, his business manager, and Gerónimo de Agüero, his former tutor.

Other loyal Colombistas met him at Santo Domingo - his uncle by marriage, Francisco de Garay, whom he named alguacil mayor, and Bartolomé's criados, Miguel Díaz, Diego Velázquez, and Juan Cerón. His coming represented the permanent establishment of the most titled and notable family in the islands, at least for many years."

In 1511, a royal council declared Hispaniola, Puerto Rico, Jamaica, and Cuba under Diego's power "by right of his father." However, Uraba and Veragua were deemed excluded, since the council regarded them as being discovered by Rodrigo de Bastidas.

The council further confirmed Diego's titles of Viceroy and admiral were hereditary, though honorific.

Furthermore, Diego had the right to one-tenth of the net royal income. However, factions soon formed between those loyal to Diego and Ferdinand's royal officials. Matters deteriorated to the point that Ferdinand recalled Diego in 1514. Diego then spent the next five years in

Spain "pointlessly pressing his claims." Finally, in 1520, Charles restored Diego's powers.

Diego returned to Santo Domingo on 12 November 1520 during a native revolt against Spanish rule in the Franciscan missions on the Cumana River, which was the site of Spanish slave raids, alongside the salt and pearl trades.

Diego sent Gonzalo de Ocampo on a punitive expedition with two hundred men and 6 ships.

Then in 1521, Diego invested in Bartolomé de las Casas' enterprise to settle the Cumana area. That failure, blamed on Diego, meant the loss of the king's confidence. That loss, plus Diego's defiance of royal power on_Cuba, forced Charles to reprimand Diego in 1523 and recall him back to Spain.

The first major slave rebellion in the Americas occurred in Santo Domingo on 26 December 1522, when enslaved Jolof laborers working on Diego's sugar plantation started a revolt.

During the rebellion, many formerly enslaved insurgents managed to escape into the mountainous interior of the colony, where they established independent maroon communities amongst the surviving

Taíno. However, a lot of rebels were captured, and the Admiral had them hanged.

After his death, a compromise was reached in 1536 in which his son, Luis Colón de Toledo, was named Admiral of the Indies and renounced all other rights for a perpetual annuity of 10,000 ducats, the island of Jamaica as a fief, an estate of 25 square leagues on the Isthmus of Panama, then called Veragua, and the titles of Duke of Veragua and Marquess of Jamaica.

After Columbus's death on February 23, 1526, in Spain, the rents, offices and titles in the Americas went into dispute by his descendants.

He initially planned to marry Mencia de Guzman, daughter of the Duke of Medina Sidonia., but he was forced by King Fernando to marry the king's cousin María de Toledo y Rojas, 1490 – May 11, 1549, who secured the transportation and burial of her father-in-law, Christopher Columbus, in Santo Domingo.

She was the daughter of Fernando Alvarez_de Toledo, 1st Lord of Villoria, son of García Álvarez de Toledo, 1st Duke of Alba, and his first wife María de Rojas, and had the following María Colón de Toledo, 1510, married to Sancho Folch de Cardona, 1st Marquess of Guadalest

Luis Colón, 1st Duke of Veragua

Cristóbal Colón de Toledo, c. 1510 – 1571, married firstly to María Leonor Lerma de Zuazo, without issue; married secondly to Ana de Pravia, and had one son, Diego Colon y Pravia,c. 1551 - Jan 27, 1578, and one daughter (Francisca Colon y Pravia, c. 1552 - April 1616]; and married thirdly to María Magadalena de Guzmán y Anaya, and had:

Diego Colón de Toledo, father of Diego the 4th Admiral of the Indies.

Francisca Colón de Toledo y Pravia c. 1550 – April 1616, married Diego de Ortegón, c. 1550, and had four children: Guiomar de Ortegon y Colon [d. 1621]; Jacoba de Oretgon y Colon, d. 1618; Ana de Ortegon y Colon; and Josefa de Ortegon y Cn.

María Colón de Toledo y Guzmán, c. 1550, married to Luis de Avila, and had:

Cristóbal de Avila y Colón, 1579, unmarried and without issue

Luis de Avila y Colón, 1582-1633, married Maria de Rojas-Guzman Grajeda, without issue; married secondly to Francisca de Sandoval and had one son Cristobal.

Juan Colón Davila, 1622, married Leonor Luyando y Manuel and had three sons.

Bernardino Davila y Colón 1633

Maria de Avila y Colón, 1592, married Alonso de Guzman Grajeda and had one daughter, Mayor de Grajeda y Avila c.1611

Magdalena Dávila Colón, 1592-1621

María Dávila Colón, 1596

Juana Colón de Toledo, died c. 1592, married her cousin Luis de La Cueva y Toledo; their only child was María Colón de la Cueva c. 1548-c.1600, who claimed the duchy of Veragua and died in New Spain, México.

Isabel Colón de Toledo c. 1515, married Dom Jorge Alberto de Portugal y Melo 1470, 1st Count of Gelves who married secondly; his 1st marriage to Dona Guiomar de Ataíde remained childless, son of Dom Álvaro de Bragança, Lord of Tentúgal, Póvoa, Buarcos and Cadaval and Chancellor-Major of the Realm of Portugal.

Their grandson, D. Nuno Alvares Pereira Colón y Portugal, Duke of Veragua and Admiral of the Indies became regent of the Kingdom of Portugal from 1621 until his death.

CHAPTER 24

Ferdinand Columbus

Ferdinand Columbus, Spanish: Fernando Colón also Hernando, Portuguese: Fernando Colombo, Italian: Fernando Colombo. He was born on August 24, 1488, and died on July 12, 1539.

He was a Spanish bibliographer and cosmographer, the second son of Christopher Columbus, Cristóbal Colón. His mother was Beatriz Enriquez de Arana, whom his father never married.

Ferdinand Columbus was born in Córdoba, Spain on August 24, 1488, the son of Christopher Columbus and Beatriz Enríquez de Arana. He had one brother, Diego Columbus, from his father's earlier marriage.

Ferdinand's parents never married, possibly because the Arana family lacked the social standing that was important to Columbus's ambitions.

Fernando's illegitimacy was never an impediment to his advancement. His father legally recognized him, and contemporary social norms were tolerant of children born out of wedlock.

When Ferdinand was born, Columbus was not yet the famous explorer, spending much of his time at the royal court of Ferdinand II of Aragon and Isabella I of Castile where he hoped to gain their support for his proposed voyage across the Atlantic to the Indies.

Meanwhile, Fernando and his brother Diego were raised by Beatriz and her family in Cordoba for the next few years. When Columbus returned from his first voyage in 1493, he instantly won fame and honors.

In March 1494, Ferdinand and his brother were presented at court in Valladolid where they were appointed to serve as the followers of Prince Juan, a significant honor, and a sign of their father's standing at court.

Although Ferdinand had only a minor role in a retinue of more than two hundred persons, he did benefit from the education that was provided for the prince and his court.

He received training in theology, Latin and Spanish grammar, history, philosophy, and music. Instruction was provided by notable humanists and theologians including Antonio de Nebrija and Peter Martyr d'Anghiera.

Ferdinand excelled in his studies and may have become something like an apprentice to Peter Martyr. After the young prince died unexpectedly in 1497, Ferdinand became a page for Queen Isabella, enabling him to continue with his education.

In 1500, Fernando's father returned from his third voyage, under arrest for mismanagement of the colony at Hispaniola. The Crown called it a misunderstanding and ordered his immediate release, but it was clear that his standing at court was at a low point.

Anxious to lead a fourth voyage and redeem his reputation, he worked with Fernando and the Carthusian monk Gaspar Goricio to assemble a manuscript called the_Book of Prophecies, Libro de las profecias.

It was an eclectic collection of biblical texts, quotes from ancient authorities and commentaries designed to show that Columbus's work was part of God's design to spread Christianity and recapture Jerusalem.

Fernando had a hand in development of the text, but the extent of his contributions has been widely debated.

By 1502, Columbus won approval from the Crown for a fourth voyage with the goal of finding a western route to the Indian Ocean. Fernando, at age thirteen, accompanied his father when the small fleet of four ships left Cadiz on 9 May 1502.

Fernando's role on this voyage is not known, but he retained his position as a royal page and received a daily allowance of 164 maravedís, an extravagant sum for a thirteen-year-old page.

This fourth and final voyage turned out to be the most dangerous and difficult. While exploring the Central American coast from Honduras to Panama, they were beset by storms, disease, mutiny, and battles with hostile natives.

After losing one ship, they attempted to return to Hispaniola for much needed repairs, but another storm marooned them on Jamaica where they waited for a year before being rescued and brought to Hispaniola in August 1504. Fernando and his father embarked for Spain in September 1504.

When they reached Seville in November 1504, Fernando remained to care for his father who was extremely ill. The expedition had been a failure, and later that month they received word that Isabella had died. It was a blow for both father and son because the queen had been their most important patron.

In May 1505, Columbus died. Contrary to popular legend, Fernando's father was not a pauper when he died but a wealthy man. The brothers inherited a sizable estate and Diego, as the first-born son, received his father's titles and privileges. However, the extent and value of these honors was very much in doubt and would require years of litigation.

Fernando did not return to court after his father's death. Instead, he focused his efforts on the legal battles to enforce the agreements with the crown that granted to Columbus and his descendants extensive rights and privileges in the Americas.

Diego would be the primary beneficiary, but Fernando felt it was a matter of family honor and loyalty. The first series of lawsuits and petitions, known as the pleitos colombinos began in 1508 and lasted until 1536.

In July 1509 Fernando accompanied Diego to Hispaniola when his brother had been named governor. Fernando remained only a couple of months and then returned to Spain to continue the lawsuits on behalf of the family.

As an adult, Columbus was known as a scholar. He had a generous income from his father's American land and used a sizeable fraction of it to buy books. Columbus travelled extensively around Europe to gather books, eventually amassing a personal library of over 15,000 volumes.

This library was patronized by educated people in Spain and elsewhere, including the Dutch philosopher Erasmus.

The impressively large library was unique in several ways.

First, Columbus personally noted each book that he or his associates acquired by listing the date of purchase, the location and how much was paid. Columbus had his associates prepare summaries of each book in his collection and devised a hieroglyphic blueprint of his library.

In 2013, history professor Guy Lazure serendipitously stumbled upon the massive catalog, known as the Libro de los Epítomes, long thought lost and consisting of 973 leaves of paper, while conducting unrelated research.

Secondly, he sought to take advantage of a recent technological development by devoting the bulk of his purchases to printed books instead of manuscripts. As a result, the library acquired a sizeable number, currently 1,194 titles, of incunabula, or books printed in the years 1453–1500.

Third, he employed full-time librarians who, as the scholar Klaus Wagner noted, were required to live on the premises to ensure that their top priority would be the library itself.

Ferdinand Columbus inherited his father's personal library. What remains of these volumes contains much valuable information on Christopher Columbus, his interests, and his explorations.

Provisions were made in Ferdinand Columbus's will to ensure that the library would be maintained after his death, specifically that the collection would not be sold and that more books would be purchased.

However, his nephew who inherited the collection took no interest in it and left it abandoned for five years in Maria de Toledo.

Even once the collection was transferred from Maria de Toledo, first to San Pablo and then to the Seville Cathedral, Ferdinand's second choice for inheritance of the books, the collection fell victim to destruction during the Inquisition as well as poor storage conditions.

During this time of disputed ownership, the library's size was reduced to about 7,000 titles. This gradually was reduced to fewer than 4,000 books, around a quarter of the initial library. However, what remains of Ferdinand Columbus's library continues to be maintained at the Seville Cathedral.

Today, a part of the Bibliotheca Colombina, it is accessible for consultation by scholars, students, and bibliophiles alike.

The Libro de los Epítomes or book of summaries of Columbus' collection was found and identified in the Arnamagnæan Collection at the University of Copenhagen in 2013.

Ferdinand Columbus was also a large-scale collector of old master prints and popular prints. More remarkable than the size of his collection, though at some 3,200 prints it is large, is the catalogue with meticulous descriptions that he had his secretaries make. This survives, although the collection itself has long gone, presumably dispersed at an early date.

This manuscript catalogue was published by Mark P. McDonald in 2004, with a single volume monograph the next year.

Columbus wrote a biography of his father in Spanish that was translated into Italian, Historie del S. D. Fernando Colombo; nelle quali s'ha particolare, & vera relatione della vita, & de fatti dell'Ammiraglio D. Cristoforo Colombo, suo padre: Et dello scoprimento ch'egli fece dell'Indie Occidentali, dette Mondo Nuovo the life of the Admiral Christopher Columbus by his son Ferdinand.

In the first paragraph of page 3 of Keen's translation, Columbus dismissed the fanciful story that his father descended from the Colonus mentioned by Tacitus. However, he refers to "those two illustrious Coloni, his relatives".

According to Note 1, on page 287, the two "were corsairs not related to each other or to Christopher Columbus, one being Guillame de Casenove, nicknamed Colombo, Admiral of France in the reign of Louis XI". At the top of page 4, Columbus listed Nervi, Cugureo, Bugiasco, Savona, Genoa, and Piacenza. all inside the former Republic of Genoa, as possible places of origin.

He also stated:

Colombo... was really the name of his ancestors. But he changed it to make it conform to the language of the country in which he came to reside and raise a new estate.

The publication of Historie has been used by historians as providing indirect evidence about the Genoese origin of his father.

Columbus's manuscript was eventually inherited by his playboy nephew, Luis, who was always short of money and sold the manuscript to Baliano de Fornari, "a wealthy and public-spirited Genoese physician".

On page xv, Keen wrote, "In the depth of winter the aged Fornari set out for Venice, the publishing center of Italy, to supervise the translation and publication of the book".

On page xxiv, the 25 April 1571 dedication by Giuseppe Moleto states:

Your Lordship, Fornari, then, being an honorable and generous gentleman, desiring to make immortal the memory of this great man, heedless of your Lordship's seventy years, of the season of the year, and of the length of the journey, came from Genoa to Venice with the aim of publishing the aforementioned book ... that the exploits of this eminent man, the true glory of Italy and especially of your Lordship's native city, might be made known.

Fernando Colón died at Seville in 1539 and is buried in the Cathedral of Seville.

CHAPTER 25

María Álvarez de Toledo

María de Toledo or María Álvarez de Toledo was born in 1490 and died on May 11, 1549. She was a Spanish noblewoman and Vicereine.

María was a substitute of the Spanish Colony of Santo Domingo on Hispaniola, present day Dominican Republic. She was the most powerful and highest-ranking noble in America in the 16th century. she was also a defender of the liberties of the indigenous people in the Hispaniola.

Maria de Toledo was granddaughter of García Álvarez de Toledo, 1st Duke of Alba and niece of Fadrique Álvarez de Toledo, 2nd Duke of Alba, cousin of King Ferdinand II of Aragon "The Catholic".

She was married to Diego Columbus, the son of Christopher Columbus. Her spouse was viceroy of the Spanish colony of Hispaniola. They resided in Alcazar de Colon in Santo Domingo.

During the absence of her husband from 1514 until 1520, she was left in charge of the colony along with Jerónimo de Agüero.

In 1523, when Diego was recalled a second time, she was named vireina. She was then expecting their eighth child.

María Colón de Toledo, 1510 –, married to Sancho Folch de Cardona, 1st Marquess of Guadalest

Luis Colón, 1st Duke of Veragua

Cristóbal Colón de Toledo, 1510 – 1571, married firstly to María Leonor Lerma de Zuazo, without issue; married secondly to Ana de Pravia, and had one son, Diego Colon y Pravia c. 1551 - Jan 27, 1578, and one daughter, Francisca Colon y Pravia, 1552 - April 1616; and married thirdly to María Magadalena de Guzmán y Anaya, and had:

Diego Colón de Toledo, father of Diego the 4th Admiral of the Indies.

Francisca Colón de Toledo y Pravia, c. 1550 – April 1616, married Diego de Ortegón, 1550, and had four children: Guiomar de Ortegon y Colon [d. 1621]; Jacoba de Oretgon y Colon [d. 1618]; Ana de Ortegon y Colon; and Josefa de Ortegon y Colon.

María Colón de Toledo y Guzmán, c. 1550, married to Luis de Avila, and had:

Cristóbal de Avila y Colón, 1579 –), unmarried and without issue

Luis de Avila y Colón (1582-1633), married Maria de Rojas-Guzman Grajeda, without issue; married secondly to Francisca de Sandoval and had one son Cristobal

Juan Colón Dávila (-1622)

Bernardino Dávila y Colón (-1633)

Maria de Avila y Colón (1592-), married Alonso de Guzman Grajeda and had one daughter, Mayor de Grajeda y Avilam, .1611

Juana Colón de Toledo (died c. 1592), married her cousin Luis de La Cueva y Toledo; their only child was María Colón de la Cueva (c. 1548-c.1600) who claimed the duchy of Veragua and died in New Spain (México).

Isabel Colón de Toledo (c. 1515 –), married Dom Jorge Alberto de Portugal y Melo (1470 –), 1st Count of Gelves (who married secondly; his first marriage to Dona Guiomar de Ataíde remained childless), son of Dom.

Álvaro de Bragança, Lord of Tentúgal, Póvoa, Buarcos and Cadaval and Chancellor-Major of the Realm of Portugal. Their grandson, D. Nuno Alvares Pereira Colón y Portugal, Duke of Veragua and Admiral of the Indies became regent of the Kingdom of Portugal from 1621 until his death.

CHAPTER 26

Plaza Colón

P laza Colón is the main plaza in the city of Mayagüez, Puerto Rico. This plaza and its fountain commemorate the explorer Christopher Columbus, whose name in Spanish was Cristóbal Colón.

The plaza presents the traditional urban relationship in Puerto Rico with the church, now Nuestra Señora de la Candelaria Cathedral on one end of the plaza and the "Alcaldia" or Mayagüez town hall in the other. Its location was designated in 1760 close to the city founding.

The plaza is covered in marble is decorated by a group of lampposts in bronze that date over more than one hundred years. Each lamp is held by an oriental figure, including characteristic clothes, turbans, and veils.

The plaza was designed after the Great Fire of 1841, approximately in 1842; years later, after being paved the plaza had a fountain in the center.

The plaza has been remodeled several times including when Benjamin Cole was mayor and under the current mayor José Guillermo Rodríguez.

Following the theory that Columbus landed in Mayagüez; in 1896 a statue of the Admiral was placed in the main plaza in the city; thus, it came to be known as Plaza Colón. The statue was made by A. Coll y Pí in Barcelona in 1843.

In 1944 a monument to the city founders was constructed in the plaza.

In 1944 Regino Cabassa made great efforts to get the creation of a Monuments to the founders of the city in the Plaza Colon. At first there were some obstacles especially since the monument was to be built of bronze and because of World War II that metal was hard to come by.

Finally on November 19, 1944, the monument was unveiled before Mayor Don Manuel A. Barreto.

More about the statue...

Columbus facing west and standing on top of a globe of the Earth, with the North and South America parts facing west also. He is standing next to a flagstaff crowned by a small cross, in which the colors of Castille and Leon are attached to.

He's raising his eyes as to thank God for his discovery. His left arm is extended, palm facing up. Since this statue is similar to that at the Plaza de Colón in San Juan there's an old running joke in Puerto Rico -well known in both cities- saying that any difficult or impossible task will only happen "cuando Colón baje el dedo"

""once Columbus lowers his finger", meaning never, since the statue usually outlives the speaker.

At the statue's pedestal you have the following art bits:

West, front, some sort of wreath, also cast from bronze, most probably a triumphal one made from olive 'branches'.

The statue is surrounded by a few fountains, which encircle the pedestal. These fountains are rather controversial, since the original plaza from 1893 didn't have them, but the remodeling have tried to "recreate the original layout of the plaza", including various side sculptures, as sculptures of Renaissance youth, either bare-breasted young females or Romeo-like dressed young men.

They were also cast by the foundry that made the original Columbus statue. Some people consider them to be distracting enough as to distort the plaza's main pattern.

Mayagüez is relatively close, 16 km or so away, from the most probable point where Christopher Columbus landed when he reached Puerto Rico in 1493. Some historians claim that Mayagüez was the actual landing site, but the evidence tends to point repeatedly that he landed at the nearby town of Aguada.

Nevertheless, Mayagüez is the larger population center in the area, and as such, features the "Plaza de Colón" with the Columbus statue. Dedicated 19 November 1892 in commemoration of the Fourth Centenary of his landing near this place in 1493.

The local Roman Catholic cathedral is behind the statue, the orange and yellow church with the two bell towers.

The Mayagüez City Hall, which very closely resembles that of New York City, but is a bit smaller is in front.

The plaza has been remodeled twice in the last thirty years, and the municipality again in January 2004, since the trees around the statue are uprooting some of the floor slabs.

CHAPTER 27

Columbus's Statue Runs
Around Puerto Rico

It would be the tallest structure in the Caribbean and among the tallest statues in the world, a monument to Christopher Columbus in a region where he has not been regarded highly for many years.

So far, though, the nearly 300-foot, 92-meter, statue of The Great Explorer just seems like a monumental morass or perhaps a colossal joke.

Originally intended to grace the skies of a major U.S. city, it has been shuffled from one locale to another and lies in pieces as a businessman and the mayor of the small Puerto Rican town of Arecibo try to finally erect it overlooking the Atlantic Ocean on the island's north coast.

But this still may not be the final chapter in what has so far been a 20-year saga. The statue's final resting place is far from certain: Its backers must gather a long list of permits, including from the Federal Aviation Administration, to install a monument so tall it could interfere with air traffic.

Now, Puerto Rican officials are competing to bring it to their parts of the island as a lure to tourists.

Then there is the fact that the roughly 600-ton, 544-metric ton, statue, like many other large-scale public works, inspires more criticism than awe, especially since Columbus is commonly viewed now as the harbinger of genocide rather than the discoverer of the New World.

"To be honest, it's a monstrosity," says Cristina Rivera, a longtime activist against the creation of private beaches in Arecibo who has been vocal about her opposition to erecting a giant Columbus in her town. "Why do we have to bring such an exaggerated piece of work here?"

It's just that kind of reaction that has doomed the project in the past and could do so again.

Russian artist Zurab Tsereteli, 77, built the statue in 1991 to commemorate the 500th anniversary of Columbus' 1492 arrival in the Western Hemisphere.

The artist is internationally renowned for giant, expensive and sometimes unwanted works. But his pieces have found a home in the U.S. before, including in front of the United Nations headquarters in New York, and he remains confident his rendition of the Great Explorer will eventually reach a destination.

Tsereteli, in an email interview with The Associated Press, notes that even the Statue of Liberty and the Eiffel Tower faced criticism and challenges.

"Now they are symbols," he said. "Without those symbols, those places would be unimaginable."

During a visit to Russia in 1990, U.S. President George H. W. Bush stopped by Tsereteli's studio in Moscow and picked one Columbus model out of three presented to him. In September 1994, Tsereteli traveled to the U.S. with then-Russian President Boris Yeltsin and presented the chosen model to President Bill Clinton.

South Florida was one of the first proposed locations for the statue, which features Columbus with shoulder-length hair, an unusually sharp and straight nose and large and slightly protruding eyes reminiscent of a Cubist painting.

One county commissioner joked it would make a good artificial reef while another suggested they could just display the head and not bother with the rest of the statue.

Some also worried about erecting something that would pay homage to a person associated with slave trading and brutal colonization.

The statue then made its rounds through New York, Ohio, and Maryland, with no success.

"Various private organizations said they would put it up," said Emily Madoff, Tsereteli's spokeswoman. "Then they realize what's involved in something so big. ... You just don't plunk it on top of the land."

In 1998, Puerto Rican Gov. Pedro Rosello accepted it as a gift and spent $2.4 million in public funds to bring it to the island. Then the mayor of Catano, a suburb of San Juan that draws thousands of tourists to its Bacardi rum distillery, requested the statue.

The plan ran into trouble when aviation authorities said the proposed location would interfere with flight paths, and residents whose homes would have to be demolished to make way for the statue protested the plans. Then Columbus went into storage. "It was awful, really awful," Madoff said. "It just sat there."

In 2008, a port management company, Holland Group Ports Investments, agreed to take the statue and store it in the western coastal city of Mayaguez, where it remains.

A Russian crew recently flew there and ensured that most of the 2,700 pieces still fit together as plans seemed to move forward in Arecibo.

Arecibo Mayor Lemuel Soto says the statue would add to the glamour of the town, which draws people to its limestone caves and one of the world's largest telescopes. Madoff says funding should not pose a problem, that investors have the $20 million it would take to erect the statue.

Now that the permit process is under way, a new threat has emerged. Puerto Rican Rep. David Bonilla has begun lobbying to put up the statue to lure tourists to the western corner of the U.S. territory, perhaps on the island of Desecheo, which is uninhabited except for the occasional errant Dominican migrant trying to escape the U.S. Border Patrol.

San Juan Mayor Jorge Santini, an influential figure on the island, also has weighed in, saying he wants Columbus in the capital. Santini envisions it near a popular lagoon or even atop an old landfill.

The artist's spokeswoman insists it's too late to start looking for a new site and that Columbus will rise in Arecibo.

CHAPTER 28

Beatriz Enríquez de Arana

Beatriz Enríquez de Arana was born about 1465 or 1521. She was the mistress of Christopher Columbus and mother of Ferdinand Columbus, Columbus's natural son, whom he later officially recognized.

Beatriz was born in the small village in Santa Maria of Trassierra, near Córdoba, into a family of peasant farmers and small shareholders. She had two brothers.

According to historian Rafael Ramírez de Arellano, her father or stepfather was Pedro de Torquemada of converso origin, and her mother was Ana Núñez de Arana.

In his story of Cordoba, he explained that Beatriz and her brother Peter took the name of their maternal aunt Mayor Enríquez de Arana. She was one of the relatives who took them with Francisco Enriquez de Arana, a wine maker, when they became orphaned in 1471.

The Núñez de Arana families were small landholders of modest means. Beatriz knew how to read and write, an unusual thing at the time, which indicated that she had at least some status in society.

Most historians agreed that the lower social status of Beatriz is the reason why Columbus never married her. He always wanted a woman of higher degree to help benefit him his ventures.

In 1479, Columbus traveled to Lisbon. He went to conduct trades and to visit his brother. That is where he met and married Filipa Moniz about 1479 or 1480. They had a son and him named Diego.

Columbus' wife died in 1484, according to some historians; others guessed that he may have simply deserted her. He took their child. At that time, Diego was about five years old. They moved to Spain.

In early 1486, Columbus was living in the court of the Spanish monarchs in Seville. This the time was trying to convince them to finance his "Enterprise of the Indies". King Ferdinand V and Queen Isabella I were preoccupied at the time trying to unify Spain.

They were interested in Columbus's idea but couldn't give it their full attention while the war in Granada was going on against the Moors. Meanwhile, Columbus was given subsistence and allowed to stay at the monarchs' castle in Cordoba as his project promised the possibility of future riches and spread of Christianity.

While waiting for their decision and another meeting with the Spanish monarchs, Columbus patronized a local pharmacist shop that was operated by people from Genoa, Italy, his probable birthplace.

At the pharmacy he became friends of a young Basque man named Diego de Arana.

Diego had two orphaned cousins in his family's household: Beatriz Enríquez de Arana and her brother Pedro Enríquez de Arana.

Diego introduced Beatriz, then 20 or 21 years old, to the 35-year-old Columbus in 1487.

In August 1488, they had a son named Ferdinand, Hernando Colon, but did not marry. Diego's family, who adopted Beatriz, had a prosperous wine business. They may have helped Columbus with money for his expeditions.

When Columbus left for his first expedition to the New World, the two children, Diego, and Ferdinand, were turned over to Beatriz. The care she gave them was noted and praised by Queen Isabella.

Some historians think that the award money intended for the look-out man that would be the first to spot land went instead to Columbus's mistress.

When Columbus died, he left some provision for her in his will, directing his son Diego to hold her in respect and continue an annual allowance.

Diego appears to have been a bit negligent with payments. Beatriz' last recorded act in 1521 was to hire an attorney to collect some money. Diego's will have to be again written in 1532 to contain that any unpaid monies from the last three or four years were to be paid out to Beatriz' heirs.

Neither her cause of death, or the exact date have been recorded, but it is assumed to have taken place shortly after 1521.

CHAPTER 29

Christopher Columbus's Descendants

Columbus's journeys were funded by the King and Queen of Spain, King Ferdinand, and Queen Isabella, who hoped that he would find gold.

As historians reported, "Columbus enjoyed a substantial revenue from Hispaniola gold during the last years of his life." After Queen Isabella, his chief patron, died, "he repeatedly attempted, unsuccessfully, to gain an audience with King Ferdinand, whom he felt owed him further compensation."

Columbus had two sons, one born of his 1478 marriage to Doña Felipa Perestrello e Moniz, and the other an illegitimate son born to Doña Beatriz Enriquez.

In his estate, Columbus left titles and income to his sons, and relations between his legitimate and illegitimate families reportedly remained cordial.

Columbus's immediate descendants brought a series of lawsuits, known as the "Pleitos Colombinos," against the Crown of Castile in the early 1500s.

The BBC reports that the lawsuits lasted for more than 20 years. Columbus's family sued for access to profits and property promised to

Columbus for his discovery, arguing that the crown didn't hold up its end of the bargain.

Luis, Columbus's grandson, won some privileges, including titles as the Duke of Veragua, and Marquis of Jamaica.

What did the royal family owe Columbus's descendants?

As PR Newswire reports, "The royals agreed, in writing, known as the 'Capitulations of Santa Fe,' to give Columbus and his heirs 'ten percent of all the wealth he discovered and claimed for the Crown on his voyages made on their behalf,' as well as land grants, extravagant titles and untold potential powers in the New World, in permanence."

The contract would reportedly be valued at more than $100 trillion in today's currency. It would have made Columbus's family one of the wealthiest families in history, if not the single richest family ever.

Newswire noted, "Columbus fell out of favor, and the Royal's revoked on their agreement."

In 1536, Columbus's heirs were awarded land in the Caribbean, in Jamaica and Hispaniola, now Haiti and the Dominican Republic. They received other powers, titles, and compensation.

Additionally, the Chicago-based Voelker Litigation Group reported that "A separate, but related, and very colorful action was brought in the form of a declaratory judgment to declare the rightful primary heirs to Columbus' legacy of money, power, and titles. This litigation continued and off for over two more centuries."

Does he have any living descendants?

Christopher Columbus does have living descendants including Cristóbal Colón, whom the BBC characterizes as the "20th Christopher Columbus" on the family tree.

Colón "dedicates most of his time to activities related to his ancestor and has represented Spain as an ambassador for special missions related to Columbus," the BBC reported. He also weighed in on the Pleitos Columbo's, telling the BBC that the Spanish crown did not "honor what was agreed."

All Things Interesting reports of Colón that "if the historical Columbus had been a little more careful with his contracts and demanded his share of the revenue from the New World to pass to his descendants in perpetuity.

They all were done with no standard clauses at that time. This family would have been richer than all in the world today put together."

The 20th Christopher Columbus also has some controversial opinions. He once wrote for USA Today that his famous ancestor doesn't deserve to be blamed for violence against indigenous peoples.

"We're quick to rewrite history and accuse Christopher Columbus of destroying Native Americans when the truth is so much more complex," Colon wrote. "What is happening at the hands of Columbus' attackers is political, not historical. As his direct descendant and namesake, I should know."

CHAPTER 30

The Real Story of Christopher Columbus

After Christopher Columbus discovered upon the island we know as Haiti 523 years ago, he wrote of the Taíno people who inhabited it. "They never refuse anything that is asked for. They even offer it themselves and show so much love that they would give their very hearts."

It was this supposed generosity and goodwill that Columbus thought would make it easier to conquer the giant island, with its "fine, large, flowing rivers" and forests "full of trees of endless varieties, so high that they seem to touch the sky."

Years later, the Taíno would be reduced to a tiny fraction of their population of approximately 300,000. Haiti lost 98 percent of those trees Columbus wanted.

There was nothing trivial about Columbus' violent destruction of Taíno people. While the sailor and his crew are sometimes grouped in with all the other conquest-crazy Europeans of their era, their cruelty can't be so easily pardoned and shouldn't be ignored.

Natives were regularly whipped for what Columbus considered minor offenses. Just for stealing a vegetable or animal could result in cutting off a Taino's nose, ear, or hand. The offender was sometimes forced to walk around with their severed body part in shame.

Columbus took and gifted Taíno women to his crewmen, who would violently beat and rape them. Pregnant Taíno women who were taken captive gave birth to babies who were sometimes thrown to hungry dogs.

Columbus established a business in the sale of 9- and 10-year-old Taíno girls for sexual slavery. He also kidnapped and enslaved Taínos themselves. He personally initiating the intercontinental slave trade in his voyage back to Europe.

In short, Columbus was a murderous, enslaving, sexual-abusing, dangerous colonizer to the peoples he encountered in the Caribbean.

Only two-thirds of the Taíno survived just four years after Columbus' arrival; some were killed, others capitulated to diseases. Half of the dead killed themselves rather than to live with his tyranny.

Columbus was also responsible for creating a system in which Taíno land was treated the way Taíno women were. Not that the Taíno didn't resist.

Columbus left behind 39 colonizers in the first European settlement in the Americas, which he called La Navidad, in present-day Haiti. When he returned from Spain several months later, he found that all the Europeans were dead. That didn't stop him.

Columbus' practice of settling on other peoples' lands in the Americas sparked the European imagination, and those lands would soon be the backbones of empires.

What followed was centuries of oppression. Spain cleared land for massive tobacco plantations, beginning a long process of deforestation and soil erosion.

After France came into possession of Haiti, it cleared even more land, and brought in enslaved Africans to cultivate sugar to satisfy European palates.

The first place Europe settled in the Americas also became the first place that successfully revolted against it. The destructive practice of monocropping for overseas consumption had already taken hold.

We shouldn't forget that Columbus is responsible for introducing an ecocide as well as a massacre. The wealth from resources like sugar, tobacco, and cotton ushered in the start of the Industrial Revolution, which began emitting carbon at an unprecedented record level.

Haiti remains the poorest country in all the Americas. The European Union region remains one of the wealthiest in the world. This isn't because of some natural curse in Haiti. It is because its peoples, their labor, their lands, and their resources have long been stolen without reparation.

The dangerous nature of the colonization of the Americas, which started in Haiti, not only terrorized the people who lived there at the time. It also created a system that kept indigenous peoples in slavery or perpetual poverty, while Europe relished in wealth.

You can tell your friend, why so many of us roll our eyes at the idea of celebrating Columbus Day.

CHAPTER 31

Columbus and Sex Trafficking

I n 1492 Columbus sailed the ocean blue" is the beginning of a poem children have been taught for generations about the Spanish explorer's landing in the Caribbean.

Columbus never set foot in mainland North America, however, his expedition is worshipped throughout the U.S. Every second Monday in October, Spain's "discovery" of the "American" continent and its peoples are celebrated as a national holiday.

Over the past six decades, organized opposition from Native people and allies regarding the accuracy about Columbus's expedition has called attention to brutality unleashed on the continent. its people will never forget Columbus and the Europeans that arrived after his initial voyage.

I have researched the business ventures that Columbus led. His first order of business was to send four sailing ships back to Europe, loaded to capacity with 550 Natives that were auctioned off in Mediterranean markets.

An international law called the Doctrine of Discovery enabled Columbus to make three expeditions to conquer non-Christian people and their territories.

In 1493, after the 'discoveries' made by Columbus, Pope Alexander VI issued a papal decree that indicated more explicitly that only Christian rulers could legitimately claim land ownership.

The result: a centuries-long process of attempted genocide and colonization of Indigenous people, including the enslavement of 2.5 to 5 million Indigenous people, death of Indigenous people from disease and murder, dismemberment, rape, land theft, destruction of animals and natural resources, starvation, removal, concentration camps, and forced religious conversion.

In combination with forced, unfair, and unfulfilled treaties, the pre-contact Indigenous population who resided in the land that is now the U.S. was ultimately reduced by 90 percent.

Less known is that Columbus and his men raped, abducted, traded, and sold for sex Indigenous women and girls. According to Columbus's notes, men "seized about five women each as their concubines, while others marauded across the island in search of villages with gold."

Columbus wrote about the Taino, the first Indigenous people he encountered. "A hundred castellanoes, Spanish coin, are as easily obtained for a woman as for a farm ... there are plenty of dealers who go about looking for girls. Those from nine to ten years old are now in demand."

As more European men invaded and enslaved the people living in what would come to be called Central and North America, most Native slaves were women and children, with women being valued at 50 to 60 percent more than men.

Historian Andres Resendez, author of "The Other Slavery," a 2016 National Book Award finalist, writes that sexual exploitation and reproductive capabilities were part of the higher price paid for Native women. He adds, "Indian slavery constitutes an obvious antecedent to the sex traffic that occurs today."

A more accurate phrasing, then, of the mantra for schoolchildren might be: In 1492 Columbus sailed the ocean blue, becoming the first known sex trafficker of the Americas, which became a central component of U.S. colonization.

CHAPTER 32

Columbus One of History's Worst Monsters

Oct. 14 is Columbus Day this year. If you celebrate Christopher Columbus, born Cristofor Colombo, on that day or any other day, you are a celebrator of racist massacre, massive land robbery, barbaric slavery, child/adult serial rape, and systemic torture.

It has been exactly 527 years since Christopher Columbus arrived on the Bahamian island of what he referred to as San Salvador on Oct. 12, 1492.

The first official Columbus Day was celebrated in 1792 in New York by the notoriously corrupt Tammany Hall on the 300th anniversary of his fictitious arrival in America. One hundred years later, President Benjamin Harrison issued a 400th anniversary proclamation.

In 1937, President Franklin D. Roosevelt proclaimed Columbus Day a national holiday.

By the way, Columbus didn't "discover" America or the so-called New World. In fact, Red/Brown people, Taino, Arawak, and Lucayan, were living on this land and in the so-called New World 14,000 years before his 1451 birth.

After Columbus' arrival in 1492, he sailed to what he labeled Espanola, which is today's Haiti and the Dominican Republic.

In the incompetent belief that he had discovered a shortcut to India. But he was thousands of miles off course. In fact, the only reason the indigenous red people in this country are commonly but erroneously called "Indian" is that he mistakenly thought he was in India and therefore arrogantly, like Europeans do, imposed a name on them.

By the way, the correct name is Ongweoweh....

Not long after his incompetent Gilligan's Island-type arrival/ invasion, and to get more royal financing from Spanish King Ferdinand and Queen Isabella, he returned to them with his exciting, but fake, news that he had found a quick route to Asia.

Accordingly, he received funding to lead three more voyages to the so-called Americas, occurring in 1493, 1498 and 1502.

As a result of those voyages, and in addition to destroying ancient civilizations, he murdered approximately eight million Red/Brown people, raped and tortured millions of them, and robbed them of millions of acres of land.

Here are five factually irrefutable and historically documented facts that prove Columbus is one of the worst- and arguably the worst- monster in world history:

Columbus ignored the King and Queen's order that he "abstain from doing, the inhabitants any injury."

For example, he created in 1495 the "tribute system" requiring every person over 14 to provide him with a "hawk's bell" of gold every three months. Those who complied were given a "token" to wear around their neck.

Those who didn't comply, as Columbus' son Fernando reported, were "punished by having their hands cut off" and "left to bleed to death."

About 10,000 in Haiti and the Dominican Republic were victimized. Many of the indigenous people were while alive "roasted on spits, slender pointed rods, and burned at the stake" and the invaders "chopped the children into pieces."

Also, Columbus' men "tore the babes from their mother's breast by their feet and dashed their heads against the rocks …

They 'splitted' the bodies of other babies, together with their mothers … on their swords."

As noted by Spanish historian and Catholic priest Bartolome de las Casas, who witnessed much of the carnage, Columbus, in order "to test the sharpness of their blades," directed his men "to cut off the legs of children who ran from them." His crew would "pour … people full of boiling soap" and cause others to be "eaten alive by hunting dogs."

If Columbus' brigade ran out of meat for their vicious dogs, "Arawak babies were killed for dog food."

A Columbus shipmate, Miguel Cuneo, wrote that "When our ships were to leave for Spain, we gathered … 1,600 male and female 'Indians' …

On Feb. 17, 1495, and we let it be known that any of the sailors who wanted to take them, could do so." Cuneo took a teenage "Caribbean girl as a gift from Columbus." And when she "resisted …, he thrashed her mercilessly and raped her."

Speaking of rape, it was noted by University of Vermont history professor Dr. James Loewen that "As soon as the 1493 expedition got to the Caribbean … Columbus was rewarding his lieutenants with native women to rape.

In Haiti, sex slaves were one more requirement that … they enjoyed." It included adult rape and child rape. As Columbus himself wrote in 1500, "… girls … from 9-10 … are … in demand."

In one day, de las Casas saw Columbus' soldiers "dismember, behead or rape 3,000 natives." As a result, de las Casas wrote, "My eyes have seen these acts so foreign to human nature that now I tremble as I write."

Columbus' evil was so efficient that when he arrived in Haiti, the Dominican Republic, and other Caribbean islands in 1493, there were 8 million Taino. That number, within a mere three years, was reduced to just 3 million.

By the time he left in 1504, only about 100,000 remained alive.

Columbus not only pioneered a new form of mass murder, but he also pioneered a new form of slavery, which he transformed into a race-based and generational form of brutal labor.

In fact, as documented by Dr. Loewen, "Columbus not only sent the first slaves across the Atlantic, but he also probably sent more slaves about 5,000 than any other individual."

Columbus' evil was so outrageous that Governor Francisco De Bodadilla, based on the testimony of 23 eyewitnesses! They arrested Columbus for inhuman and widespread crimes against the Taino/Arawak/Lucayan population and shipped him back to Spain in shackles.

The evidence was so overwhelming that Columbus confessed and was convicted.

Instead of celebrating on Oct. 14 one of the worst and arguably the worst monster in world history, ask some of this country's wonderful Italian Americans for a list of the names of some of the world's greatest Italians and Italian Americans.

I'm sure that list would feature hundreds, including Amerigo Vespucci first European to recognize North and South America as distinct continents and to realize unlike Columbus that the so-called New World was not part of Asia, Antonio Santi Giuseppe Meucci identified by the U.S.

Congress as the real inventor of the telephone and Guglielmo Marconi Nobel Prize-winning electrical engineer and physicist who is validly credited as the inventor of the radio.

Italians and Italian Americans don't like racist monsters. Red people, Brown people, Black people and other people of color don't like racist monsters either. In fact, we hate them and therefore don't celebrate them.

CHAPTER 33

Columbus Day or Indigenous Peoples' Day

Columbus Day began as a celebration of Italian immigrants who faced persecution in the U.S. For many, it's now a symbol of the colonization and oppression of Indigenous people.

Was Christopher Columbus a heroic explorer or a murderer? It depends on who you ask. The fight over how or whether the United States should commemorate the Italian navigator's 1492 landing in the Americas has increased controversy for generations.

A federal holiday celebrated the second Monday of each October, Columbus Day arose out of a late 19th century movement to honor Italian American heritage at a time when Italian immigrants faced widespread persecution.

The holiday has since come under fire as a celebration of a man whose arrival in the Americas signaled the oppression of another group of people: Native Americans. In recent decades, it has been replaced by Indigenous Peoples' Days in many states and cities.

In 2021, the U.S. celebrated its first national Indigenous Peoples' Day in a commemoration President Joe Biden proclaimed as a day to honor "our diverse history and the Indigenous peoples who contribute to shaping this, Nation.

"Biden also issued a Columbus Day proclamation acknowledging the contributions of Italian Americans as well as "the painful history of wrongs and massacres" that resulted from European exploration. Here's how Columbus Day began, and how the movement to replace it has gained momentum.

On October 12, 1492, after a voyage of 10 weeks, Christopher Columbus' crew spotted the New World. The Italian navigator's three ships, sailing at the request of the Spanish crown, would soon land, likely on an island known to its Lucayan residents as Guanahaní. Columbus christened it San Salvador.

It was the beginning of a new era in the history of the Western Hemisphere, an event commemorated in the U.S. since the nation was founded in 1776.

Before the late 19th century, the celebrations were mainly limited to Catholic and Italian American enclaves on the East Coast, where many embraced Columbus as an intrepid explorer who embodied progress and bravery.

For these people, Columbus represented their permanent contribution to a society that viewed both Catholics and Italian Americans with suspicion.

Celebrations of Columbus gained momentum as Italian immigration grew from a trickle to a flood. Beginning in the 1880s, Italian immigrants began pouring into the U.S. in search of opportunity and a better life. But the new arrivals were not welcomed by all.

Maligned as sinister and criminal, Italian immigrants were the focus of increasing racism.

In 1890 anti-Italian sentiment boiled over in New Orleans after police chief David Hennessy, reputed for his arrests of Italian Americans, was murdered. In the aftermath, more than a hundred Sicilian Americans were arrested.

When nine were tried and acquitted in March 1891, a furious mob rioted and broke into the city prison, where they beat, shot, and hanged at least 11 Italian American prisoners.

None of the rioters who lynched the Italian Americans were prosecuted. It remains one of the largest mass lynchings in the nation's history.

The brutal killings created tit-for-tat tensions between the U.S. and Italy, which called for reparations for the murders.

At first, the U.S. refused, prompting Italy to recall its ambassador, and cut off diplomatic relations. The U.S. reciprocated.

Eventually, to satisfy Italy and acknowledge the contributions of Italian Americans on the 400th anniversary of Columbus' arrival, President Benjamin Harrison in 1892 proclaimed a nationwide celebration of "Discovery Day," recognizing Columbus as "the pioneer of progress and enlightenment."

Eventually, the nations mended their relationship and the U.S. paid $25,000 in reparations.

In the decades after the mass lynching, Italian American advocates pushed for a nationwide holiday, and states slowly began to adopt it. In 1934, President Franklin D. Roosevelt designated it a national holiday, and in 1971 Congress changed the date from October 12 to the second Monday of October.

The holiday, writes historian Bénédicte Deschamps, "allowed Italian Americans to celebrate at the same time their Italian identity, their Italian American group specificity, and their allegiance to America."

Columbus Day is celebrated by all the Italians. For many with Indigenous ancestry, it was a slap in the face, a celebration of invasion, theft, brutality, and colonization.

Columbus and his crew enabled and perpetrated the kidnapping, enslavement, forced assimilation, rape and sexual abuse of Native people, including children; the Native American population shrank by about half after European contact.

For Indigenous Americans, the landing celebrated by some as a day of triumphant discovery was the beginning of an incursion onto land that had long been their home.

In the 1960s and 1970s, the Pan-Indian and Red Power movements brought together Native Americans who began to draw attention to the hero's sordid history.

In 1970, for example, anonymous protesters scrawled Red Power slogans on the statue of the navigator in the middle of New York's Columbus Circle ahead of Columbus Day celebrations.

The New Yorker reported on the incident, calling it "a topic to joke about safely" among white politicians on the viewing stand for that day's festivities an indication of just how far the movement would have to go to change the nation's view of Columbus.

In the 1980s and 1990s, protests the holiday grew...

In 1990, ahead of the 100th anniversary of the Wounded Knee Massacre, in which U.S. soldiers killed some 300 Lakota people, Native American publisher Tim Giago urged South Dakota's governor to declare it a year of reconciliation and change Columbus Day to a holiday called Native American Day.

The governor, George S. Mickelson, agreed, and the holiday has replaced Columbus Day in the state ever since.

Two years later, ahead of the 500th anniversary of Columbus' landing, Indigenous groups lobbied the United Nations and local governments not to participate in international celebrations.

A group called Resistance 500 formed in the Bay Area in response to the plans such as an event in which replicas of Columbus' ships sailed into San Francisco Harbor.

Berkeley's city council recognized the group as a task force and unanimously adopted its suggestion of replacing Columbus Day with a holiday called the Day of Solidarity with Indigenous People.

The Indigenous activists won another victory when the ships' journey was called off in the face of growing pressure.

Though Italian American groups protested the move, it fueled ongoing activism among Indigenous people. In the 2010s, Indigenous Peoples' Day, known by some as Native American Day, gained steam as it was adopted by scores of cities and states around the nation.

Some states honor both Columbus Day and Indigenous Peoples' Day on the paid holiday, while others have renamed it entirely.

In addition, multiple states have stopped celebrating the date altogether. According to Pew Research, in 2021 only 21 states offered their government workers paid holidays on the second Monday in October.

Even Columbus, Ohio, the largest city named after the Italian navigator, has changed its tune: In 2018, it stopped celebrating Columbus Day, and in 2020 it declared October 12 Indigenous Peoples' Day.

"It's impossible to think about a more just future without recognizing these original sins of our past," Columbus City Council president Shannon Hardin reportedly said at the meeting.

In a similar spirit of reckoning, in April 2019 New Orleans Mayor LaToya Cantrell apologized for the 1891 lynchings of Italian Americans, more than a century after the incident.

CHAPTER 34

The Royal family owe
Columbus's Descendants

The royals agreed, in writing, known as the 'Capitulations of Santa Fe,' to give Columbus and his heirs 'ten percent of all the wealth he discovered and claimed for the Crown on his voyages made on their behalf,' as well as land grants, extravagant titles and untold potential powers in the New World, in perpetuity.

The contract would reportedly be valued at more than $100 trillion in today's currency.

It would have made Columbus's family one of the wealthiest families in history, if not the single richest family ever.

Columbus fell out of favor, and the Royal's defaulted on their agreement." In 1536, Columbus's heirs were awarded land in the Caribbean, in Jamaica and Hispaniola, now Haiti and the Dominican Republic, other powers, titles, and compensation.

Additionally, the Chicago-based Voelker Litigation Group reports that "A separate, but related, and very colorful action was brought in the form of a declaratory judgment to declare the rightful primary heirs to Columbus' legacy of money, power, and titles. This litigation continued, on and off, for over two more centuries.

Christopher Columbus does have living descendants, including Cristóbal Colón, whom the BBC characterizes as the 20th Christopher Columbus on the family tree.

Colón "dedicates most of his time to activities related to his ancestor and has represented Spain as an ambassador for special missions related to Columbus.

He also weighed in on the Pleitos Colombinos, the Spanish crown did not honor what was agreed.

All Things Interesting reports of Colón that if the historical Columbus would have been a little more careful with his contracts and demanded his share of the revenue from the New World to pass to his descendants in perpetuity, which was a standard clause at the time, he would have been richer than all the other people in the world today put together.

The 20th Christopher Columbus also has some controversial opinions. He once wrote in an op-ed for USA Today that his famous ancestor doesn't deserve to be blamed for violence against indigenous peoples.

"We're quick to rewrite history and accuse Christopher Columbus of decimating Native Americans when the truth is so much more complex," Colon wrote." What is happening at the hands of Columbus' detractors is political, not historical. As his direct descendant and namesake, I should know."

CHAPTER 35

Remains of possible Descendants of Christopher Columbus

A national investigation is trying to prove that the explorer was from Pontevedra in the Spanish province of Galicia through genetics.

An investigation, which is based on the 'Galician Theory' hopes to prove the idea that Christopher Columbus was originally from the Pontevedra, has begun this week with the first excavations.

On the first day, seven bones, ceramics and other objects have been recovered after reaching a depth of 32 inches in the old cemetery of San Salvador de Poio.

The work at another, the San Martiño de Sobrán cemetery, in Vilaxoán-Vilagarcía de Arousa, has been complicated and will take longer than initially planned.

Since the researchers have found them on land where cement had been poured on top of the first layer, this is making the work harder.

Colón Gallego association, the University of Granada and the production company Story Producciones participate finds this complicated.

The fact that the excavations are not as deep as could be expected has led researchers to believe that the earth was likely removed at some point for the transfer of the cemetery to the new location, which is why tombs have changed place more recently.

Additionally, beyond the four bones found seven different bones. This indicated that the coffins from previous exhumations and pottery have not yet been dated.

The president of the Colón Gallego Association, Eduardo Esteban, explained to the press that there had been a "technical problem" in the opening of the grave of Juan Mariño de Sotomayor.

Professor José Antonio Llorente, one of the project's researchers, will not travel to open the coffin.

Columbus was Galician because "there is a lot of documentation" that supports it...

The idea that Christopher Columbus was from Galicia, specifically from Poio, Pontevedr, is a "serious and consolidated" theory that, over the years, has been endorsed with "a lot of documentation," according to Esteban.

The investigations in the old cemetery of Poio are due to the "reasoning" that the Columbus clan must be buried there, whose prescence in Portosanto is known on the basis that if they lived there, they will be buried in that place.

"It has been proven that he could be Galician because the documentation that exists is overwhelming," one of the main defenders of the Galician origin of the historic Spanish conqueror once again told the press on Wednesday. "There is more than reliable evidence", he insisted.

To these indications, the experts added that Columbus wrote numerous annotations and letters in Galician or that many of the names of places that were discovered on that expedition correspond to local names of places on the coast of Galicia.

"We are closer than ever", assured Esteban, to refuting the rest of the theories that suggest that the discoverer of America could have been born in Genoa, Italy, Barcelona or Mallorca.

CHAPTER 36

The Love and Hate for Christopher Columbus

The "explorer" of America has gone from hero to villain in just a few years. His figure characterizes the debate on how we interpret the past.

In 2020, a year after Mexican President Andres Manuel Lopez Obrador demanded that Spain apologize for the abuses of the Conquest of America, the statue of Christopher Columbus was dismantled from the Paseo de la Reforma in Mexico City.

It was a kind of preface to a wave of monument removals in honor of the Italian-born navigator which exploded with the Black Lives Matter movement.

Spain celebrates its National Day on October 12. At the center of the controversy, and object of many of the reactions, is the figure of the Italian sailor, who led the first great European expedition that set foot on American soil for the first time on October 12, 1492.

In the last decade, capitals such as Bogota in Colombia, La Paz in Bolivia and Argentina's Buenos Aires have gotten rid of their Columbus statues; many of these countries celebrate October 12 as Columbus Day.

In the United States, with more than 40 statues removed since 2018, it has been renamed Indigenous Peoples Solidarity Day and, in many states, no longer equates to a holiday. In Caracas, Venezuela, the statue of Columbus was pulled down in 2004 as a symbol of genocide.

Today obtaining certainties about the figure of the explorer has become a journey. History has long said Columbus 'discovered' the New World for Spain, and in doing so it set in motion a chain of events that led to the brutal suppression of indigenous peoples across the Americas.

The terms such as <u>presentism</u>, cancel culture and the so-called woke generation are making historical reinterpretation, with all its challenges, the norm. What certainties do we have left?

Presentism has always existed

<u>Presentism</u> is the phenomenon that explains the vandalized statue of slaveholder Edward Colston in Bristol, or the dismantling of the monument to secessionist General Lee in Richmond in Virginia, U.S., to cite just two examples.

Understood as the analysis of past events from the moral rules of the present, <u>presentism "is nothing new"</u> according to Richard Kagan, Professor Emeritus of history at John Hopkins University, U.S., since, for centuries, historians have selected their topics according to contemporary issues and concerns. "In light of the importance the current news cycle accords to issues relating to race, climate, gender, social and economic inequalities on a global scale," Kagan says, "many of today's historians seek to offer new perspectives on these issues in the past, whether recent or remote."

It is a fact that, outside Spain, the public image of Columbus has been degraded over the years. Also in the Spanish educational system, the subject recently caused controversy when a high school philosophy textbook asked students whether "the Spanish State should assume responsibility for colonialism". One might ask: Has Columbus always been studied as a conquering hero?

One must go back to the biography of Christopher Columbus published in 1828 by Washington Irving to find the first foundations that shaped the glory of heroism around Columbus.

"He was presented as a progressive and forward-looking individual determined to overcome the liberalism and backwardness represented by the professors of Salamanca who questioned, rightly, as it turned out, his calculations about the size of the globe", notes Kagan.

It was only in the second half of the 20th century that historians used a variety of new archival sources to begin to pay attention to other facets of Columbus's trajectory, "thus chipping away at the heroic image Irving did so much to create," Kagan concludes.

Kagan believes that preserving the statues teaches students the reasons why they were erected in the first place, "it's impossible to erase the past, it's better to learn from it", and suggests that, in California, attacks and acts of vandalism on the statues of Juan de Oñate in Albuquerque and San Junipero Serra in California "have gone too far."

It is "better to use these statues teaching as tools to learn about the past and especially about societies whose values, ideas about race and religion, and women as well, were markedly different from those of today."

Somewhere between the two extreme points of view, Israel Alvarez Moctezuma, Professor of Medieval Studies at the Faculty of Philosophy and Letters of the UNAM, Mexico, believes that "cancelling the past is an exercise in collective amnesia where we still do not know what consequences it will have.

The statues of Columbus and the English slavers should not be in public space, but in a museum, because they are undeniably part of our history, however painful it may be."

For Fernando Cervantes, Mexican historian, and professor of Modern Age studies at the University of Bristol, branding Columbus as a hero means "uncritically accepting the advances of the theory of progress according to which Columbus was part of the rationalist and practical trajectory that laid the foundations of the scientific revolution and the Enlightenment".

Cervantes strikes down as a "blatant myth" the idea that Columbus was a character ahead of his time and fighting against diehard and superstitious views of the world, as well as the idea, "still widely accepted", that Columbus's contemporaries opposed his plans because they thought the world was flat.

The Deadly Impact

Even though Columbus never set foot in North America, in July 2020, the speaker of the California Assembly ordered the removal of the monument erected in 1883 to Christopher Columbus and Isabella the Catholic arguing that it was "a deeply polarizing historical figure given the deadly impact his arrival in this hemisphere, the West, had on indigenous populations."

Is historical revisionism more topical than ever or has it always been present in one form or another?

For Matthew Restall, ethnohistorian and professor of Latin American history and anthropology at the Pennsylvania State University, US, the nuance is very subtle.

Historical writing has always been revisionist, especially the best historical scholarship. However, the awareness of History's revisionist nature waxes and fades, and I do agree that today there is more awareness of it.

The key to understanding the real Columbus is to separate him from the many Columbuses that were invented after his death and continue to be invented. Hero and villain are just two of those inventions," Restall says via e-mail.

"The more Columbus is made a symbol of momentous historical events, the more he is going to attract passionate defenders and detractors... Thus, the battles over statues, monuments, and day names are not really about Columbus, but about myriad other issues."

In the late 1990s, moved by the accumulation of misunderstandings he found in the beliefs of his students, Restall wrote the book Seven Myths of the Spanish Conquest:

"I realized that most of them had picked up misconceptions about the larger topic, from Columbus to the Aztecs and conquistadors to the larger history of European imperialism in the Americas, and that those misconceptions, or myths as I came to call them, were rooted in what historians had written during the previous century, which was in turn rooted in what Spaniards and other Europeans had written during the imperial centuries 16th to 19th".

In his work, Restall elaborates on the idea that the villain is not the person, but the concept: "the idea, embraced by millions of people, that it is justifiable for one group of people to invade, massacre, exploit and enslave another group."

He also sheds light on the, at the time, non-existent Spanish nationality, the belief that the conquest was executed under the orders of Ferdinand II of Aragon, the fundamental help of indigenous allies in the expansion of the empire.

The fact that there were territories that were never conquered, amongst other topics. "The more Columbus is made a symbol of momentous historical events, the more he is going to attract passionate defenders and detractors.

Thus, the battles over statues, monuments, and day names, Columbus vs Indigenous Peoples, are not really about Columbus, but about myriad other issues", he stated.

Using history as a weapon

Restall puts the spotlight on the fine line that, once crossed, turns historical revisionism, "which strictly follows the rules of evidence", into distorted manipulation of the historical method in the service of presentist political objectives: "Although there are many others, the most egregious example is Holocaust denial."

Historical revisionism "is not only positive, but also essential," says Emilio Redondo, professor of American History at the Complutense University of Madrid.

"There is no definitive historical truth, it is always provisional", says Redondo, also stressing the importance of nuance:

"The fact that there is now a greater sensitivity to unedifying behaviors that a century ago were overlooked in great historical figures should not be censured or disqualified as mere presentism. Just as they should not be exposed to public mockery or thrown into the sink of silence".

Redondo highlights how in Spain the concept of historical revisionism has been tainted with certain pejorative connotations, especially in the biased study of the Second Republic, the Civil War and Francoism.

This sense, Redondo places the discovery of America and the "publishing boom related to the Hispanic imperial past" as another example of instrumentalized narratives:

"It is very significant that here the revisionist phenomenon has been produced in a double aspect: on the one hand, the uncritical glorification of that imperial past; on the other, its unmitigated condemnation from a presentist vision.

"It is in this scheme where the game between Americophilia's and apeirophobia's that we suffer today fits, and that generally does not start from the honest will to understand the past, but from the justification of ideological positions in the present".

Proof of this is, for example, the existence of symposiums organized by dozens of researchers who claim that Columbus was in fact Catalan or at least spoke it according to Estelle Irizarry, a researcher at Georgetown University, U.S.

"Responsible historical revisionism would be that which seeks to tell the story and the experience of the greatest possible number of people, groups and collectives, offering a plurality of perspectives on a given moment in our past, without giving preeminence to any of them."

OLIVIA MUÑOZ-ROJAS

Although the role of the Internet and social networks in the pursuit of freedom of expression is unquestionable, Redondo highlights the "paradox that these same social networks that have opened up public debate are the ones that provoke censorship or at the very least, vituperation of different opinions – under the protection of anonymity and gregariousness that characterize these digital mass media".

Cancel culture and the woke generation

According to the Oxford English Dictionary, which added the term into its 2017 edition, the adjective 'woke' alludes to a person who is 'alert to racial or social discrimination and injustice.'

The word, paradoxically, came with the inclusion of another no less sensitive term: post-truth.

Used pejoratively by, among others, former U.S. President Donald Trump, to mock the captain of the U.S. women's soccer team, the word woke has become a weapon of choice for conservatism or a title to be proud of.

It was coined by The New York Times in 1962, and in recent times we have seen it associated with the outbreak of social movements related to race, gender, and sexual orientation, among other issues.

Pilar García Jordan, professor of Modern and Contemporary History at the University of Barcelona, believes that historical revisionism is more present today "due to the spread of the woke culture in Europe and, with it, the progressive imposition of a uniform and unique thought."

Garcia Jordán adds the matrix of this thought is "found in North American society; a culture that has built a theoretical framework, alien to European culture, which has been imported by some sectors of a certain, political] left".

García Jordán believes that, by assigning a political configuration based on people's identities, "the class struggle is becoming a struggle of identities".

The professor claims that the woke culture has fostered the so-called cancel culture, which "based on a supposed idea of the common good, promotes not only the suppression of the individual or the need for individual actors, representatives of public and private institutions to ask forgiveness for events and processes that took place hundreds of years ago," she says, adding: "but also, in the name of the so-called political correctness, is intended to annul dissenting voices that are subjected to scorn and harassment."

She cites as an example the British philosopher Kathleen Stock who, after being accused of transphobia, left teaching at the University of Sussex in 2021.

For Dr. Kelly Elizabeth Wright, experimental sociolinguist in Language Sciences at Virginia Tech, U.S., change is innate to people, language and life "there will never be a world with certainties" and the only thing we can do is "take actions that tend towards kindness", and then make it clear that "leaving statues of individuals known to have caused discrete harm to communities seeking relief from that harm is not something that tends towards kindness".

Wright is convinced that nothing is immutable and draws a parallel between the evolution of language and its use to explain realities.

Wright asserts that all so-called non-normative individuals, whether LGBTQ, disabled or homeless, have been kept out of all official meaning-making processes for the entire history of print until about 200 years ago: "White people named the heavens.

They named all the parts of the body. They named all the places and the things and the stuff in their own image and not that of the people's necks they stood upon, whose lands they spoiled.

Historical revisionism is almost all there has ever been. When you ask me why are we seeing people pulling statues down and refusing to celebrate those who slaughter, if these acts are coherent? I must ask you: what are you called to do when you learn that you have been lied to?"

So, are we condemned to live a perpetual revision of past events to help us better understand the present? Have we entered a revisionist spiral that will feed back on itself until the end of time?

Alejandro de la Fuente, Professor of Latin American History and Economics at Harvard University in the U.S. believes that such a spiral has always existed, and that the current situation, both in academia and in the media, is that realities "have to compete with other narratives that also circulate in the public space; there are more opportunities to think about history from other experiences and from other political projects".

In the opinion of Olivia Muñoz-Rojas, PhD in Sociology from the London School of Economics, United Kingdom, "responsible historical revisionism would be that which seeks to tell the story and the experience of the greatest possible number of people, groups and collectives, offering a plurality of perspectives on a given moment in our past, without giving preeminence to any of them".

Columbus' voyages and the subsequent European conquest and colonization of America is one of the historical processes that most changed the history of mankind.

"The process that Columbus initiated in America was plagued by a brand of violence that has been perpetuated over time, reaching our days in the form of structural racism and inequality suffered by millions of people in American countries," explains Muñoz-Rojas.

What we are witnessing "is a vindication of the vanquished, the oppressed, the silenced."

But he points out, not all the conquests of the past have these consequences in the present: "I don't see many groups demanding recognition of the crimes of Pharaonic Egypt, for example, or the Roman Empire, because their consequences are less palpable in the present".

CHAPTER 37

People suddenly hating Christopher Columbus

What you're seeing is the second wave of opposition to Columbus and Columbus Day. Back in the 19th century, it was, embarrassingly, connected to anti-Catholicism, with the Klan and other Protestant and nativist movements opposing it on the grounds of connection to immigration from Catholic countries.

More recently, however, it's been in recognition of Columbus's tremendous negative impact on native peoples of the Americas, and that's been brewing for a long time.

Native Americans were never big fans of Columbus, but there's been increasing awareness of native issues among the rest of the population since the 60s, and there's been an organized movement against Columbus Day since at least 1990.

Now, more and more people are becoming aware of it, but this is in no way sudden. This is part of a movement which has been going on for a generation or more.

Here is his report of his first meeting with the indigenous people:

"They … brought us parrots and balls of cotton and spears and many other things… They willingly traded everything they owned… They were well-built, with good bodies and handsome features…. They do not bear arms, and do not know them, for I showed them a sword, they took it by the edge and cut themselves out of ignorance. They have no iron. Their spears are made of cane…. They would make fine servants…. With fifty men we could conquer them all and make them do whatever we want."

Another sailor describes his rape of a native woman "gifted" to him by Columbus.

"While I was in the boat I captured a very beautiful Carib woman, whom the said Lord Admiral gave to me, and with whom, having taken her into my cabin, she is being naked according to their custom, I conceived desire to take pleasure.

I wanted to put my desire into execution, but she did not want it and treated me with her fingernails in such a manner that I wished I had never begun. But seeing that, to tell you the end of it all, I took a rope and thrashed her well, for which she raised such unheard-of screams that you would not have believed your ears.

Finally, we came to an agreement in such manner that I can tell you that she seemed to have been brought up in a school of harlots."

Several accounts of cruelty and murder include Spaniards testing the sharpness of blades on Native people by cutting them in half, beheading them in contests and throwing Natives into baskets of boiling soap.

There are also accounts of breast-feeding infants being lifted from their mother's breasts by Spaniards, only to be dashed headfirst into large rocks.

Bartolome De Las Casas, a former slave owner who became Bishop of Chiapas, described these exploits. "Such inhumanities and barbarisms were committed in my sight as no age can parallel," he wrote.

"My eyes have seen these acts so foreign to human nature that now I tremble as I write."

Because Columbus reported an excess of Natives for slaves, rivers of gold and fertile pastures to Queen Isabella and King Ferdinand, Columbus was given 17 ships and more than 1,200 men on his next expedition. However, Columbus had to deliver.

In the next few years, Columbus was desperate to fulfill those promises, hundreds of Native slaves died on their way back to Spain and gold was not as abundant as expected.

Columbus forced the Natives to work in gold mines until exhaustion. Those who opposed were beheaded or had their ears cut off.

In the provinces of Cicao all persons over 14 had to supply at least a thimble of gold dust every three months and were given copper necklaces as proof of their compliance.

Those who did not fulfill their obligation had their hands cut off, which were tied around their necks while they bled to death and some 10,000 died handless.

In two years', time, approximately 250,000 Indians in Haiti were dead. Many deaths included mass suicides or intentional poisonings or mothers killing their babies to avoid persecution.

According to Columbus, in a few years before his death, "Gold is the most precious of all commodities; gold constitutes treasure, and he who possesses it has all he needs in the world, as also the means of rescuing souls from purgatory, and restoring them to the enjoyment of paradise."

In addition to putting the Natives to work as slaves in his gold mines, Columbus also sold sex slaves to his men. Some as young as 9. Columbus and his men also raided villages for sex and sport.

In the year 1500, Columbus wrote: "A hundred castellanoes are as easily obtained for a woman as for a farm, and it is very general and there are plenty of dealers who go about looking for girls; those from nine to ten are now in demand."

In the early years of Columbus' conquests there were butcher shops throughout the Caribbean where Indian bodies were sold as dog food. There was also a practice known as the montería infernal, the infernal chase, or manhunt, in which Indians were hunted by war-dogs.

These dogs who also wore armor and had been fed human flesh, were a fierce match for the Indians. Live babies were also fed to these war dogs as sport, sometimes in front of horrified parents.

NORMA IRIS PAGAN MORALES

After a multitude of complaints against Columbus about his mismanagement of the island of Hispaniola, a royal commissioner arrested Columbus in 1500 and brought him back to Spain in chains.

Though he was stripped of his governor title, he was pardoned by King Ferdinand, who then subsidized a fourth voyage. Myths and Atrocities About Christopher Columbus and Columbus Day - Indian Country Media Network

Historians have uncovered extensive evidence of the damage wreaked by Columbus and his teams, leading to an outcry over emphasis placed upon studying and celebrating him in schools and public celebrations.

In an era in which the international slave trade was starting to grow, Columbus and his men enslaved many native inhabitants of the West Indies and subjected them to extreme violence and brutality.

On his famous first voyage in 1492, Columbus landed on an unknown Caribbean Island after an arduous three-month journey.

On his first day in the New World, he ordered six of the natives to be seized, writing in his journal that he believed they would be good servants.

Throughout his years in the New World, Columbus enacted policies of forced labor in which natives were put to work for the sake of profits. Later, Columbus sent thousands of peaceful Taino "Indians" from the island of Hispaniola to Spain to be sold. Many died on their way there..

Those left behind were forced to search for gold in mines and work on plantations. Within 60 years after Columbus landed, only a few hundred of what may have been 250,000 Taino were left on their island.

As governor and viceroy of the Indies, Columbus imposed iron discipline on what is now the Caribbean country of Dominican Republic, according to documents discovered by Spanish historians in 2005.

In response to native unrest and revolt, Columbus ordered a brutal crackdown in which many natives were killed; to prevent further rebellion, Columbus ordered their dismembered bodies to be paraded through the streets.

CHAPTER 38

Who Discovered America?

Why did history decide that Christopher Columbus was to be the one person recognized, as the person who "discovered America"?

It's not a question of who arrived first, but who started the exchange of people, culture, and trade between continents whose people were previously unaware of each other.

Irrespective of whether there were prior voyages from Romans, Basques, Scots, Vikings, etc. arriving in America, it was Columbus voyage the only one with a transcending influence in people, trade and culture of Europe, America, and other regions. Up to then, both worlds remained distinct and isolated, ignoring each other.

Eventually Columbus voyage changed those worlds forever, something that none of the possible prior voyages did.

CHAPTER 39

Views On The Native Americans

"It is true that after they have been reassured and have lost this fear, they are so artless and so free with all they possess, that no one would believe it without having seen it.

Of anything they have, if you ask them for it, they never say no; rather they invite the person to share it and show as much love as if they were giving their hearts, and whether the thing be of value or of small price, at once they are content with whatever little thing of whatever kind may be given to them."

I found what Columbus wrote to his benefactors, Ferdinand, and Isabella, to be of particular interest.

In this quote, Columbus explains his views on the Native Americans. We see that he was shocked with what he saw. The Native Americans were kind and loving people, something he did not expect.

He discusses how they are always willing to give and never say no to someone if they need something. They are always willing to do whatever it takes to make other people happy.

Most importantly, Columbus sees that he can take advantage of the Native Americans because of their kind manner. If he is respectful to them, they will respect him.

By being respectful to them and by giving them stuff of value, he will gain their utmost respect and attention, making it easier for him to convince them to give him the goods he needs to bring back to his country.

CHAPTER 40

Different Feelings On Columbus Around The World

Americans tend to think that in 1492, when Columbus sailed the ocean blue, he claimed this land for Spain, and simply went home. But Columbus played a huge role in the history of the Caribbean, Central and South America, and Columbus Day is one of celebration and protest in Latin America.

Host Michel Martin speaks with author Timothy Kubal about how the holiday has turned from a day praising Columbus as the colonizer to the Day of Indigenous Resistance.

Next on this Columbus Day holiday here in the U.S., we turn elsewhere to look at how Christopher Columbus is regarded in Latin America.

Now, of course, most of us remember the little ditty from grade school. In 1492, Columbus sailed the ocean blue, and of course, that narrative seems to suggest that Christopher Columbus simply arrived, claimed this land for Spain and went on back home.

Columbus continued his journey, and his explorations played an important role in the history of the Caribbean and Central and South America. In fact, Columbus Day is a day of celebration and protest and reflection in Latin American countries, as well.

We wanted to know more, so we've called author Timothy Kubal. He wrote the 2008 book "Cultural Movements and Collective Memory: Christopher Columbus and the Rewriting of the National Origin Myth."

He's a professor of sociology at California State University Fresno, and he's with us now. Welcome, professor, thanks so much for joining us.

Professor TIMOTHY KUBAL, Author, "Cultural Movements and Collective Memory: Christopher Columbus and the Rewriting of the National Origin Myth": Thanks for having me.

MARTIN: So, when did Columbus Day celebrations, if that is indeed what they are, start in Latin America? And what did they look like?

Prof. KUBAL: Well, the early days of such celebrations really didn't come about until Latin American countries started to demand their own freedom from colonization.

So, we saw the Columbus Day, or Dia de la Raza is what it was traditionally called, beginning throughout Latin Americas in the early 1800s.

And it's currently that the holiday is mostly a patriotic holiday. We see similar remnants of what we see today in Spain. We see military marches, parades, which is a very conservative, patriotic type of holiday.

MARTIN: Now, you know, when a holiday is named for a person, it tends to come with a narrative. what was the narrative? And is it still the narrative of how the holiday is observed?

Prof. KUBAL: What I found is that there are many narratives, and they co-exist, certainly there's the traditional narrative. Anytime you have a, as you say, a holiday focused on an individual, you do have an opening for creating alternative narratives.

You have the importance of the colonizer, the importance of Spanish culture, and the importance of the development of the Hispanic race from the Spanish colonizers.

The other narrative, which is that mixed race, that mestizo race that developed, is primarily one of being proud of your Indian heritage.

144

That's the narrative that's become more popular in recent eras, but it coexisted even in the early years.

MARTIN: And that's what I was going to ask you is when did that start because we know, of course, you know, now there are several leftist leaders like Hugo Chavez in Venezuela, Evo Morales in Bolivia and Rafael

Correa in Ecuador who promote indigenous culture and promote indigenous pride. Did the focus on indigenous culture start before these leaders started promoting that aspect?

Prof. KUBAL: Absolutely. It points to the political nature of this holiday when we have the leaders like Morales and Chavez in particular latching onto this holiday and using it to highlight ethnic distinctions in their countries for political reasons. This is something that in fact it is not new.

The motivation for the change, for the growth of this counter-narrative that Chavez really popularized comes about in the days leading up to 1992. Spain was celebrating. Of course, everybody was celebrating.

This was the 500-year anniversary. Spain was sponsoring World's Fair in 1992, and there was a lot of pomposity about the patriotism of this day.

The groups in Mexico City and many cities throughout Latin America had started to come together around protesting this holiday. The real growth of this counter-narrative comes at about 1987 or 1988.

Starting about 1988 and up to about 1994, there was a distinct pattern of events that went on every Columbus Day. The first half of the event was a celebration of ethnic culture.

This is where they would sing ethnic songs. They would display ethnic clothes. They would share ethnic foods and stories, and they would speak in ethnic languages in the speeches.

In the second half of the event, they would often travel to a Columbus statue that was usually in the center square of the city, and they would hold a protest event, which was a much angrier rather than a celebration of an ethnic culture, this was an angry event where they talked about injustices.

They talked about the horrors of colonization and so on and so forth. They would sometimes throw rocks, eggs, and other projectiles at statues, and even in some cases, as in Venezuela, they actually tore down that statue.

MARTIN: And as we said, in 2002, Hugo Chavez declared Columbus Day to be the day of indigenous resistance, which is now an official government holiday.

Prof. KUBAL: That's right. But this was not just a name change. This was a fundamental change in the relationship between the governments and indigenous people.

Columbus Day was sort of a symbol of this, that we were going to, instead of celebrating the colonizer, we are going to celebrate the colonized. Chavez used the day to do many symbolic actions to help the indigenous people.

He announced the distribution of thousands of acres of land, along with free tractors from the government. He also kicked out Christian missionaries on Columbus Day, another symbolic act of supporting the colonized.

This holiday of the day of indigenous resistance is more than just the symbolism of a name change, but a day that's been used as a vehicle to talk about the redistribution of resources to indigenous people.

MARTIN: So that was eight years ago. How about now?

Prof. KUBAL: Much of the political fervor that existed around the holiday has really sort of waned off. Of course, still in Venezuela and Bolivia, you still see Hugo Chavez. He's got a weekly radio and television program, where he still rails against Columbus and talks about supporting decolonization. And Hugo Chavez is not the only one.

We still see some political use of this holiday, but it doesn't seem to mobilize the masses the way it used to.

MARTIN: Timothy Kubal is a professor of sociology at California State University Fresno. He wrote the book "Cultural Movements and

Collective Memory: Christopher Columbus and the Rewriting of the National Origin Myth." He joined us from member station KVPR in Fresno. Professor, thanks so much for joining us.

CHAPTER 41

Christopher Columbus
the Perfect Icon

Christopher Columbus was the Perfect Icon for a New Nation Looking for a Hero. America's love affair with Christopher Columbus has been a rocky one.

Some enjoy his day to celebrate Italian-American heritage, while others annoyed at the misconduct of honoring a man who enslaved and killed thousands of native peoples.

Our universal statues and "Columbias" testify to how passionately most of the nation once embraced Columbus. If the object of such ardor seems inappropriate in the modern world there's also ample evidence that the whole affair began rather badly not with affection for Columbus himself but with a disdain for England and the desire for a uniquely American hero.

Native Americans called these shores home for perhaps 15,000 years before Columbus arrived. Norsemen reached North America centuries before Columbus, and even his contemporaries may have reached the new world first according to this intriguing map.

In any event, Columbus never even set foot on the North American mainland, as John Cabot did in 1497.

How did Columbus become the idealized symbol of New World discovery? It didn't happen right away. For several centuries after the voyages of discovery Columbus, Cabot and other explorers were mostly bypassed by history.

"By the time Columbus dies, he's kind of a forgotten figure, as was John Cabot. Both were largely ignored within a decade or so of their deaths," says University of Bristol historian Evan Jones.

"In the mid-1700s they were mentioned in history books but as rather secondary figures, not as heroes."

The 200th anniversary of Columbus's landing in 1692 featured neither word nor deeds commemorating the explorer, according to University of Notre Dame historian Thomas J. Schlereth's 1992 study in the Journal of American History, which coincided with the 500th anniversary of the landing.

What changed? American colonists needed a heroic symbol for their new, independent nation. Columbus, albeit with some ahistorical narrative tweaks, fit the bill rather nicely. Cabot did not despite the fact he was no Englishman, but an Italian like Columbus himself.

"John Cabot is a much better person to have made much of," Bushman adds. But Cabot sailed under an inconvenient flag.

"Particularly after 1776, the Americans don't really want to associate themselves with things, including Cabot, that represent British claims to North America at a time when the United States is asserting its independence," Jones notes.

"What they like about Columbus is that at this time he's being portrayed as being almost an Enlightenment figure. He represents freedom, a guy who had turned his back on the Old World and sailed in the name of a monarch and then been treated very badly by that monarch."

Widespread accusations of colonial misgovernance led the Spanish crown to have Columbus arrested and returned to Spain in chains, where he served a short prison term. Though King Ferdinand freed him and later financed a fourth voyage Columbus's stature and power would never really recover.

"Of course, there was a resonance there at a time when Americans felt they'd been treated very badly by George III," says Jones. "It's not as if people write diatribes against Cabot or discredited Cabot. They just kind of forgot about him."

Cabot isn't forgotten everywhere. His Discovery Day is celebrated Newfoundland and Labrador, where he set foot on mainland North America. But he quickly faded from U.S. history even as Columbus began a truly meteoric rise.

By 1777, the American poet Philip Freneau described his country as "Columbia, America as sometimes so called from Columbus, the first discoverer."

There were others who advocated that the 13 states should adopt the name "Columbia" instead of the United States of America. They didn't, of course, but they did dub the nascent capital the "Territory of Columbia" in 1791.

King's College, named under the rule of George III, was renamed Columbia in 1784. South Carolina announced Columbia as its state capital in 1786.

In 1788, the Society of Tammany or Columbian Order was founded it later became the power broking machine of the Democratic Party in New York headed by 'Boss' Tweed.

"It took as its patrons Tammany, the legendary Indian chief of the Delaware tribe, and Columbus himself, these two figures being thought of as archetypically American," wrote John Larner in Proceedings of the American Philosophical Society, during the Columbus Quincentenary.

What was it about Columbus that commended him to so many during this period? Larner asserted that few Americans of the time knew much about Columbus the man:

For most patriots, I would imagine, two things sufficed. The first was that he wasn't English. The second was that, as it was believed, he had been treated with ingratitude by an Old-World monarchy.

Among the toasts drunk at the Tammany celebration of the Tercentennial - toasts played a large part in these early commemorations - was one that asked:

"May the deliverers of America never experience that ingratitude from their country which Columbus experienced from his king."

Columbus also provided a convenient way to forget about America's original inhabitants.

"In early American textbooks from the 1700s Columbus is the first chapter. Columbus starts American history," says Claudia Bushman. "There's nothing about the Indians.

In the 1700s you had to have a different way of thinking about America. Some of these books even show pictures Columbus in colonial era clothing. People had a very shaky concept even of how many years had passed."

In extreme cases, Bushman adds, Columbus has been employed to entirely obscure not only the Native American era but also the British colonies.

"There was a 20th century statue in Worcester, Massachusetts, with this great inscription detailing how wonderful it was that Columbus was 'inspired by the Lord to go forth, search for and find these United States of America.' There you've just eliminated 300 years of history," she notes.

If the cult of Columbus was always more about an ideal than the man himself, that concept found full expression in the creation of Columbia a feminine figure that came to represent the young New World nation.

This symbolic symbol appeared in newspapers, engravings, magazine titles, place and ship names, songs, and political cartoons of publications like Puck and Harper's Weekly.

The adjective Columbian was applied to stand for uniquely American virtues and graced everything from schoolbooks to learned societies like the Columbian Institute for the Promotion of the Arts and Sciences. A major influence on what later became the Smithsonian Institution. "Hail Columbia," written for George Washington's first inauguration and refitted with lyrics nine years later, was the nation's de facto national anthem until the close of the 19th century.

This female Columbia became so ubiquitous and enduring that many learned Americans no longer recognize the connection even when surrounded by examples of it.

"When I gave a seminar over the summer to a bunch of high-flying Fulbright students from the U.S., all of whom were history majors, none of them were even aware of the Columbus-Columbia connection," Jones said.

"They were fascinated by it, having grown up with 'Columbia' as a name and an icon but never really having thought about where she came from."

Where she did not come from, not really, was Christopher Columbus the man. Columbus as a historical character, rather than as a symbol, wasn't visible until Washington Irving's 1827 biography essentially re-imagined him, Bushman explains.

"That's the first time he really appears, as far as I could tell. His remaking by Washington Irving really changes the whole way he's considered. It's a beautiful whitewash job."

For those like Bushman who delve into the history behind Columbus the person, neither the humanizing Irving portrayal nor the symbolic Columbus square with the deeds of the man himself.

"It's a shock to go back and read the original documents and see that all the mean things they say about Columbus are true," Bushman says. "He was a terrible figure really, who somehow became an idealized symbol for a nation. It's simply remarkable how these things happen in history."

CHAPTER 42

The Letter

The Letter from Columbus to Luis De Sant Angel Announcing His Discovery in 1493....

As I know you will be rejoiced at the glorious success that our Lord has given me in my voyage, I write this to tell you how in thirty-three days I sailed to the Indies with the fleet that the illustrious King and Queen, our Sovereigns, gave me, where I discovered a great many islands, inhabited by numberless people; and of all I have taken possession for their Highnesses by proclamation and display of the Royal Standard without opposition.

To the first island I discovered I gave the name of San Salvador, in commemoration of His Divine Majesty, who has wonderfully granted all this. The Indians call it Guanaham. The second I named the Island of Santa Maria de Concepcion; the third, Fernandina; the fourth, Isabella; the fifth, Juana; and thus, to each one I gave a new name.

When I came to Juana, I followed the coast of that isle toward the west, and found it so extensive that I thought it might be the mainland, the province of Cathay; and as I found no towns nor villages on the sea-coast, except a few small settlements, where it was impossible to speak to the people, because they fled at once, I continued the said route, thinking I could not fail to see some great cities or towns; and finding at the end of many leagues that nothing new appeared, and that the coast led northward, contrary to my wish, because the winter had already set in, I decided to make for the south, and as the wind also was against my proceeding, I determined not to wait there longer, and turned back to a certain harbor whence I sent two men to find out whether there was any king or large city.

They explored for three days, and found countless small communities and people, without numbers, but with no kind of government, so they returned.

I heard from other Indians I had already taken that this land was an island, and thus followed the eastern coast for one hundred and seven leagues, until I came to the end of it. From that point I saw another isle to the eastward, at eighteen leagues' distance, to which I gave the name of Hispaniola.

I went thither and followed its northern coast to the east, as I had done in Juana, one hundred and seventy-eight leagues eastward, as in Juana. This island, like all the others, is most extensive. It has many ports along the sea-coast excelling any in Christendom and many fine, large, flowing rivers.

The land there is elevated, with many mountains and peaks incomparably higher than in the center isle. They are most beautiful, of a thousand varied forms, accessible, and full of trees of endless varieties, so high that they seem to touch the sky, and I have been told that they never lose their foliage. I saw them as green and lovely as trees are in Spain in the month of May. Some of them were covered with blossoms, some with fruit, and some in other conditions, according to their kind. The nightingale and other small birds of a thousand kinds were singing in the month of November when I was there.

There were palm trees of six or eight varieties, the graceful peculiarities of each one of them being worthy of admiration as are the other trees, fruits, and grasses.

There are wonderful pine woods, and very extensive ranges of meadow land. There is honey, and there are many kinds of birds, and a great variety of fruits.

Inland there are numerous mines of metals and innumerable people. Hispaniola is a marvel. Its hills and mountains, fine plains and open country, are rich and fertile for planting and for pasturage, and for building towns and villages.

The seaports there are incredibly fine, as also the magnificent rivers, most of which bear gold. The trees, fruits and grasses differ widely from those in Juana. There are many spices and vast mines of gold and other metals on this island.

They have no iron, nor steel, nor weapons, nor are they fit for them, because although they are well-made men of commanding stature, they appear extraordinarily timid.

The only arms they have are sticks of cane, cut when in seed, with a sharpened stick at the end, and they are afraid to use these. Often I have sent two or three men ashore to some town to converse with them, and the natives came out in great numbers, and as soon as they saw our men arrive, fled without a moment's delay although I protected them from all injury.

At every point where I landed, and succeeded in talking to them, I gave them some of everything I had cloth and many other things without receiving anything in return, but they are hopelessly timid people. It is true that since they have gained more confidence and are losing this fear, they are so unsuspicious and so generous with what they possess, that no one who had not seen it would believe it.

They never refuse anything that is asked for. They even offer it themselves, and show so much love that they would give their very hearts. Whether it be anything of great or small value, with any trifle of whatever kind, they are satisfied.

I forbade worthless things being given to them, such as bits of broken bowls, pieces of glass, and old straps, although they were as pleased to get them as if they were the finest jewels in the world.

One sailor was found to have got for a leather strap, gold of the weight of two and a half castellanos, and others for even more worthless things much more; while for a new blancas they would give all they had, were it two or three castellanos of pure gold or an arroba or two of spun cotton.

Even bits of the broken hoops of wine casks they accepted, and gave in return what they had, like fools, and it seemed wrong to me. I forbade it and gave a thousand good and pretty things that I had to win their love, and to induce them to become Christians, and to love and serve their Highnesses and the whole Castilian nation, and help to get for us things they have in abundance, which are necessary to us.

They have no religion, nor idolatry, except that they all believe power and goodness to be in heaven. They firmly believed that I, with my ships and men, came from heaven, and with this idea I have been received everywhere, since they lost fear of me. They are, however, far from being ignorant.

They are most ingenious men, and navigate these seas in a wonderful way, and describe everything well, but they never saw people wearing clothes, nor vessels like ours. Directly I reached the Indies in the first isle I discovered, I took by force some of the natives, that from them we might gain some information of what there was in these parts; and so, it was that we immediately understood each other, either by words or signs.

They are still with me and still believe that I come from heaven. They were the first to declare this wherever I went, and the others ran from house to house, and to the towns around, crying out, "Come ! come! and see the man from heaven!" Then all, both men and women, as soon as they were reassured about us, came, both small and great, all bringing something to eat and to drink, which they presented with marvelous kindness.

In these isles there are a great many canoes, something like rowing boats, of all sizes, and most of them are larger than an eighteen-oared galley. They are not so broad, as they are made of a single plank, but a galley could not keep up with them in rowing, because they go with incredible speed, and with these they row about among all these islands, which are innumerable, and carry on their commerce.

I have seen some of these canoes with seventy and eighty men in them, and each had an oar. In all the islands I observed little difference in the appearance of the people, or in their habits and language, except that they understand each other, which is remarkable.

Therefore, I hope that their Highnesses will decide upon the conversion of these people to our holy faith, to which they seem much inclined. I have already stated how I sailed one hundred and seven leagues along the seacoast of Juana, in a straight line from west to east.

I can therefore assert that this island is larger than England and Scotland together, since beyond these one hundred and seven leagues there remained at the west point two provinces where I did not go, one of which they call Avan, the home of men with tails.

These provinces are computed to be fifty or sixty leagues in length, as far as can be gathered from the Indians with me, who are acquainted with all these islands.

This other, Hispaniola, is larger in circumference than all Spain from Catalonia to Fuentarabia in Biscay, since upon one of its four sides I sailed one hundred and eighty-eight leagues from west to east. This is worth having and must on no account be given up.

I have taken possession of all these islands, for their Highnesses, and all may be more extensive than I know, or can say, and I hold them for their Highnesses, who can command them as absolutely as the kingdoms of Castile.

In Hispaniola, in the most convenient place, most accessible for the gold mines and all commerce with the mainland on this side or with that of the great Khan, on the other, with which there would be great trade and profit, I have taken possession of a large town, which I have named the City of Navidad.

I began fortifications there which should be completed by this time, and I have left in it men enough to hold it, with arms, artillery, and provisions for more than a year; and a boat with a master seaman skilled in the arts necessary to make others; I am so friendly with the king of that country that he was proud to call me his brother and hold me as such.

Even should he change his mind and wish to quarrel with my men, neither he nor his subjects know what arms are, nor wear clothes, as I have said.

They are the timidest people in the world, so that only the men remaining there could destroy the whole region and run no risk if they know how to behave themselves properly.

In all these islands the men seem to be satisfied with one wife except they allow as many as twenty to their chief or men. The women appear to me to work harder than the men, and so far, as I can hear they have nothing of their own, for I think I perceived that what one had others shared, especially food.

In the islands so far, I have found no monsters, as some expected, but, on the contrary, they are people of very handsome appearance.

They are not black as in Guinea, though their hair is straight and coarse, as it does not grow where the sun's rays are too ardent. And in truth the sun has extreme power here since it is within twenty-six degrees of the equinoctial line.

In these islands there are mountains where the cold this winter was very severe, but the people endure it from habit, and with the aid of the meat they eat with very hot spices.

As for monsters, I have found no trace of them except at the point in the second isle as one enters the Indies, which is inhabited by a people considered in all the isles as the most vicious, who eat human flesh.

They possess many canoes, with which they overrun all the isles of India, stealing, and seizing all they can. They are not worse looking than the others, except that they wear their hair long like women, and use bows and arrows of the same cane, with a sharp stick at the end for want of iron, of which they have none.

They are ferocious compared to these other races, who are extremely cowardly; but I only hear this from the others. They are said to make treaties of marriage with the women in the first isle to be met with coming from Spain to the Indies, where there are no men. These women have no feminine occupation but use bows and arrows of cane like those before mentioned, and cover and arm themselves with plates of copper, of which they have a great quantity.

Another island, I am told, is larger than Hispaniola, where the natives have no hair, and where there is countless gold; and from them all I bring Indians to testify to this.

To speak, in conclusion, only of what has been done during this hurried voyage, their Highnesses will see that I can give them as much gold as they desire, if they will give me a little assistance, spices, cotton, as much as their Highnesses may command to be shipped, and mastic as much as their Highnesses choose to send for, which until now has only been found in Greece, in the isle of Chios, and the Signoria can get its own price for it; as much lign-aloe as they command to be shipped, and as many slaves as they choose to send for, all heathens. I think I have found rhubarb and cinnamon.

Many other things of value will be discovered by the men I left behind me, as I stayed nowhere when the wind allowed me to pursue my voyage, except in the City of Navidad, which I left fortified and safe. Indeed, I might have accomplished much more, had the crew served me as they ought to have done.

The eternal and almighty God, our Lord, it is Who gives to all who walk in His way, victory over things apparently impossible, and in this case signally so, because although these lands had been imagined and talked of before they were seen, most men listened incredulously to what was thought to be but an idle tale.

But our Redeemer has given victory to our most illustrious King and Queen, and to their kingdoms rendered famous by this glorious event, at which all Christendom should rejoice, celebrating it with great festivities and solemn Thanksgivings to the Holy Trinity, with fervent prayers for the high distinction that will accrue to them from turning so many peoples to our holy faith; and also from the temporal benefits that not only Spain but all Christian nations will obtain.

Thus, I record what happened in a brief note written on board the Caravel, off the Canary Isles, on the 15th of February 1493.

Yours to command,

THE ADMIRAL

Postscript within the letter

Since writing the above, being in the Sea of Castile, so much wind arose south southeast, that I was forced to lighten the vessels, to run into this port of Lisbon to-day, which was the most extraordinary thing in the world, from whence I resolved to write to their Highnesses.

In all the Indies I always found the temperature like that of May. I returned in thirty-three days I returned in twenty-eight, except that these storms have detained me fourteen days, knocking about in this sea, here all seamen say that there has never been so rough a winter, nor so many vessels lost. Done the 14th day of March.

This letter Columbus sent to the Chancellor of the Exchequer, from the Islands discovered in the Indies, enclosed in another to their Highnesses.

REFERENCES

Colegio de Arquitectos de Puerto Rico (September 1984), National Register of Historic Places Inventory — Nomination Form: Plaza Publica (PDF), retrieved January 26, 2016.

National Park Service (December 13, 1985), Weekly announcement of National Register of Historic Places actions (PDF), p. 180, retrieved January 26, 2016.

Mari, Brenda A. (March 25, 2005). "Something Sweet Like Mango in the Air: A Primer on Mayagüez". PUERTO RICO HERALD. Puerto Rico: PUERTO RICO HERALD. Retrieved August 8, 2010.

"Plaza Colón" (in Spanish). Archived from the original on April 1, 2009. Retrieved 2009-07-27.

Rigau, Jorge (2009). Puerto Rico Then and Now. San Diego, California: Thunder Bay Press. p. 75.

Aguilo Ramos, Silvia (1984). Mayaguez: Nota's para su Historia. San Juan, Puerto Rico: Model Offset Printing. p. 46.

Aguilo Ramos, Silvia (1984). Mayaguez: Notas para su Historia. San Juan, Puerto Rico: Model Offset Printing. p. 46.

Archivo Nacional de Madrid, Ministerio de Ultramar (Legado 5147, Expediente 14)

"Genealogias Biografias e Historia del Mayagüez de Ayer y Hoy y Antologia de Puerto Rico"; by Martin Gaudier (Author); Page: 17; Publisher: Imprenta "El Aguila", San German (1959); Language: Spanish

"Historia de Mayagüez 1760-1960"; by Subcomite de la Historia de Mayaüez (Author); Page: 71; Publisher: Talleres Graficos Interamericanos (1960); Language: Spanish

"Historia de Mayagüez 1760-1960"; by Subcomite de la Historia de Mayaüez (Author); Page: 228-230; Publisher: Talleres Graficos Interamericanos (1960); Language: Spanish

Gilman, D. C.; Peck, H. T.; Colby, F. M., eds. (1905). "Columbus, Diego. The youngest brother of Christopher Columbus". New International Encyclopedia (1st ed.). New York: Dodd, Mead.

Floyd, Troy (1973). The Columbus Dynasty in the Caribbean, 1492-1526. Albuquerque: University of New Mexico Press. p. 31.

"Diego Columbus". Encyclopedia Britannica.

Barry, J.J. The Life of Christopher Columbus, Loreto Publications, 2017. ProQuest Ebook Central. pp. 72

The Life of Christopher Columbus from His Own Letters And Journals by Edward Everett Hale

Columbus, Ferdinand (1959). The Life of the Admiral Christopher Columbus by his son Ferdinand. New Brunswick: Rutgers, The State University. p. 175.

Francis, J. Michael (2017). Latin American History: Encyclopedia of Pre-Colonial Latin America (Prehistory to 1550s). Facts on File.

Stevens-Acevedo, Anthony (2019). The Santo Domingo Slave Revolt of 1521 and the Slave Laws of 1522: Black Slavery and Black Resistance in the Early Colonial Americas (PDF). New York, USA: CUNY Dominican Studies Institute.

Jose Franco, Maroons, and Slave Rebellions in the Spanish Territories, in "Maroon Societies: Rebel Slave Communities in the Americas", ed. by Richard Price (Baltimore: Johns Hopkins University Press, 1996), p. 35.

Miles H. Davidson (1997). Columbus Then and Now: A Life Reexamined. University of Oklahoma Press. p. 49. ISBN 9780806129341.

"GeneAll.net - Diego Colón, 1. duque de Veragua".

Inclan, John D. "The Descendants of Christopher Columbus, Admiral of the Ocean Seas".

Winsor, Justin (1891), Christopher Columbus and how He Received and Imparted the Spirit of Discovery, Chadwyck-Healey Ltd., pp. 526–527

ABOUT THE AUTHOR

Norma Iris Pagan Morales was born in Ponce, Puerto Rico. She comes from a very lovable family. Her parents, Juan Jose Pagan Rodriguez, and Digna Morales Figueroa, now deceased, always helped her with her projects as a writer and teaching career. Norma had three siblings, Adelin Milagros Pagan Morales, Juan Jose Pagan Morales, and Julio Manuel Pagan Morales. Julio Manuel Pagan Morales died on September 19, 1998, and Adelin Milagros Pagan Morales died on February 17, 2023.

Norma did all her academic studies in New York City, Puerto Rico, and Canada. She worked in the City of New York Police Department. As an Educator, she worked in New York City Bd. of Education as an English Teacher, in Puerto Rico Bd. of Education as an English teacher and in the Puerto Rico Army National.

Norma has published eleven books: Proud of My Puerto Rican Bequest, ¿Porque Soy Boricua? Poemas del Alma, Art in Written Form, A Baffling Short Stories Collection, On Job in the Big Apple, Puerto Rican Soldiers Serving with Pride, Nature's Rage in the Caribbean, Boricua de Pura Cepa, You are the One and The Unfaithfuls.

www.ingramcontent.com/pod-product-compliance
Lightning Source LLC
Chambersburg PA
CBHW021636120626
46545CB00002B/576